Time Clock

FANTAGRAPHICS BOOKS
7563 Lake City Way NE
Seattle, Washington 98115

EDITOR: *Gary Groth*
DESIGNER: *Michael Heck*
PRODUCTION: *Preston White*
ASSOCIATE PUBLISHER: *Eric Reynolds*
PUBLISHER: *Gary Groth*

To receive a free full-color catalog of comics, graphic novels, prose novels, and other fine works of artistry, including books by Leslie Stein, call 1-800-657-1100, or visit www.fantagraphics.com.

ISBN: 978-1-60699-930-1
Library of Congress Number: 2016930126

First Fantagraphics printing: June, 2016

Printed in China

TIME CLOCK

L. Stein

RON

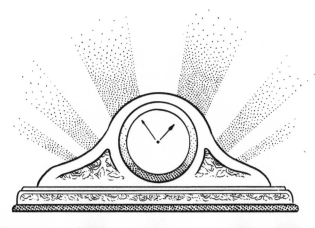

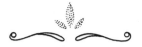

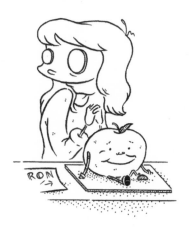

BEEP.

BEEP.

BEEP.

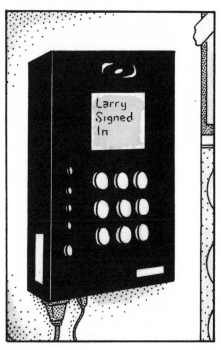

Larry
Signed
In

Hola muchachos!

Hola muchachita!

Hola sexy.

Hola!

Hola Pika!

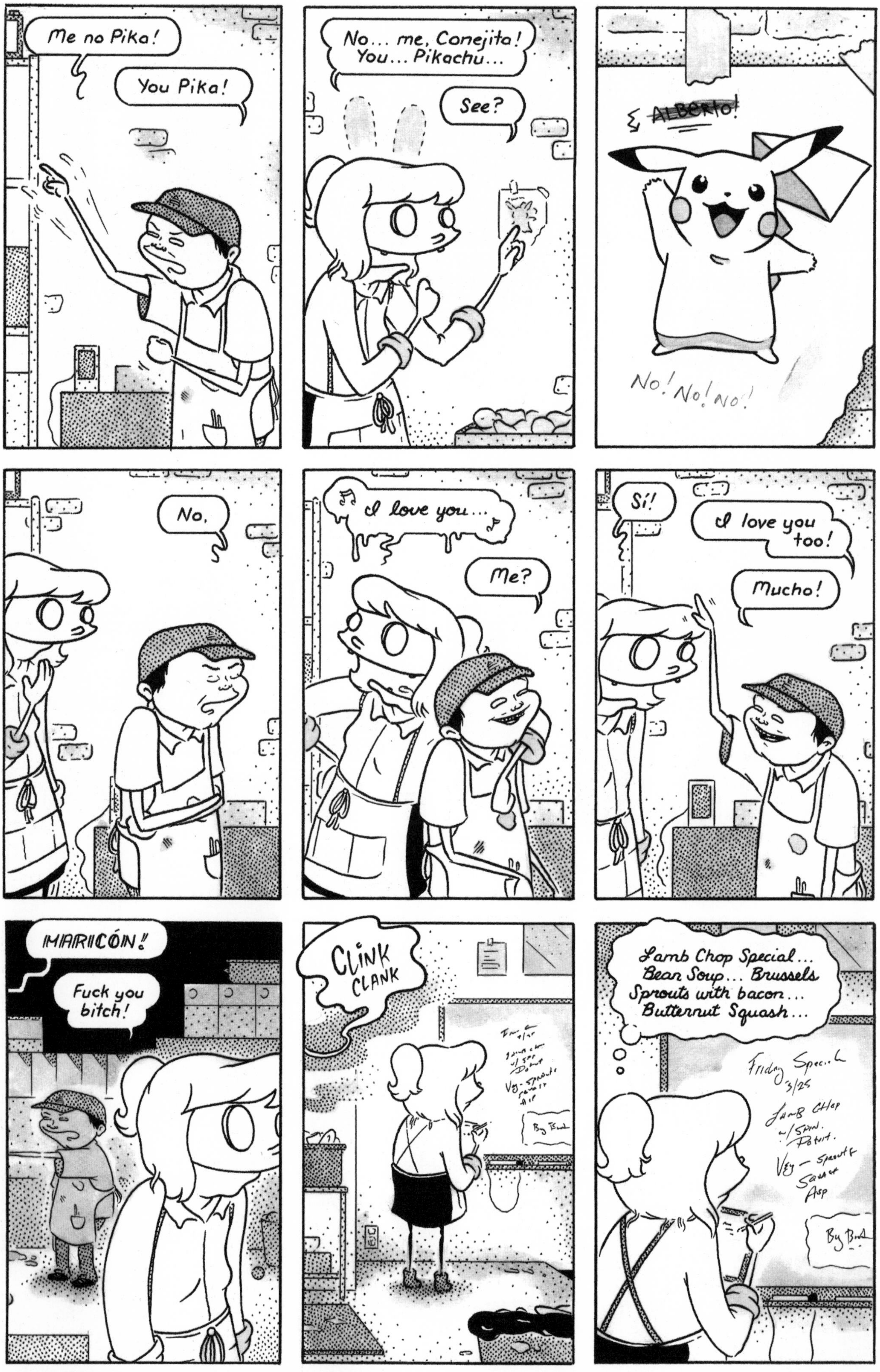
Me no Pika!
You Pika!
No... me, Conejita! You... Pikachu...
See?
¿ ALBERTO!
No! No! No!
No.
I love you...
Me?
Sí!
I love you too!
Mucho!
MARICÓN!
Fuck you bitch!
CLINK CLANK
Lamb Chop Special... Bean Soup... Brussels Sprouts with bacon... Butternut Squash...
Friday Special 3/25
By Brad

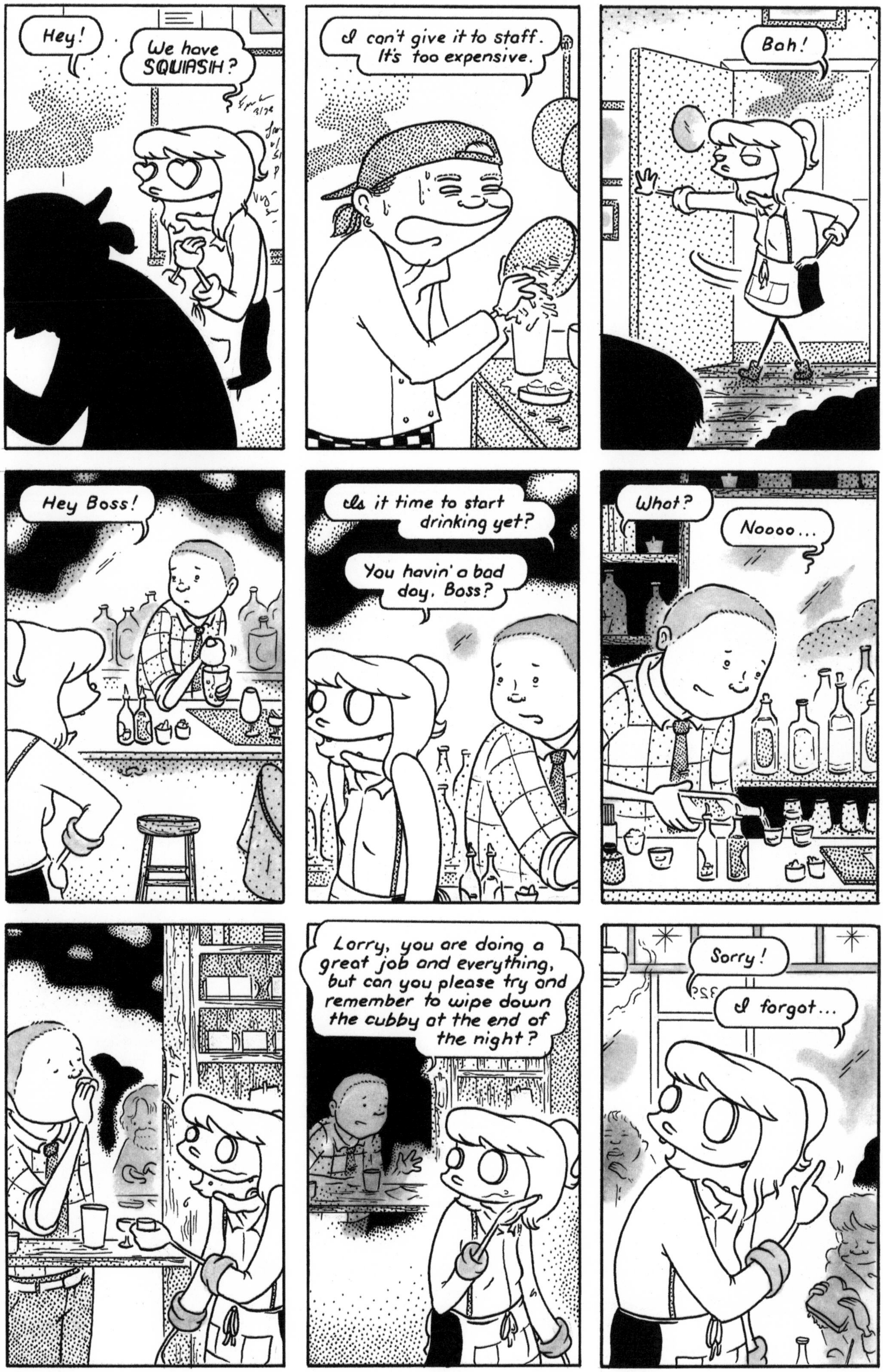
Hey!
We have SQUASH?
I can't give it to staff. It's too expensive.
Bah!
Hey Boss!
Is it time to start drinking yet?
You havin' a bad day, Boss?
What?
Noooo...
Larry, you are doing a great job and everything, but can you please try and remember to wipe down the cubby at the end of the night?
Sorry!
I forgot...

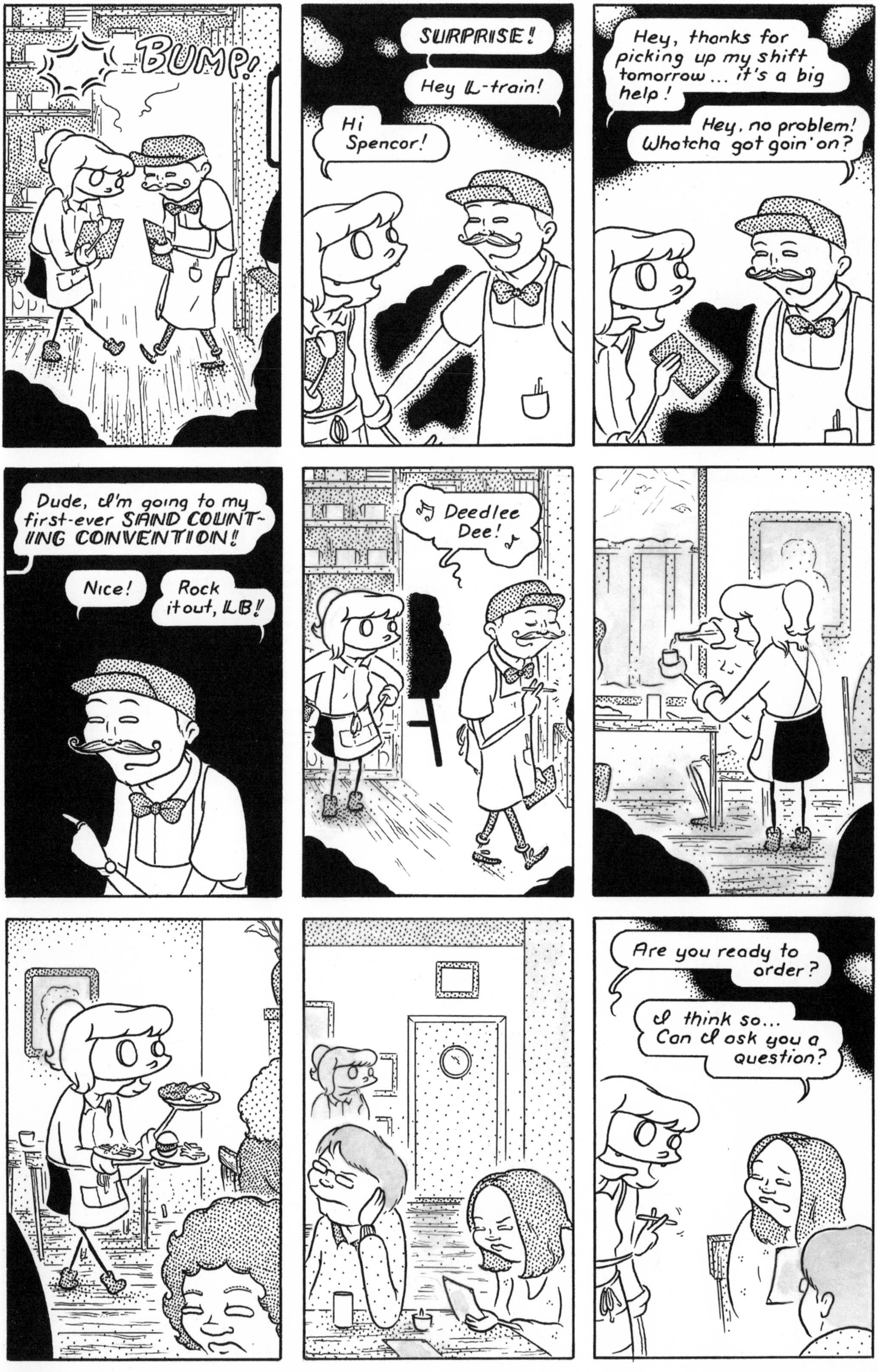
BUMP!
SURPRISE!
Hey L-train!
Hi Spencor!
Hey, thanks for picking up my shift tomorrow... it's a big help!
Hey, no problem! Whatcha got goin' on?
Dude, I'm going to my first-ever SAND COUNTING CONVENTION!
Nice!
Rock it out, LB!
Deedlee Dee!
Are you ready to order?
I think so... Can I ask you a question?

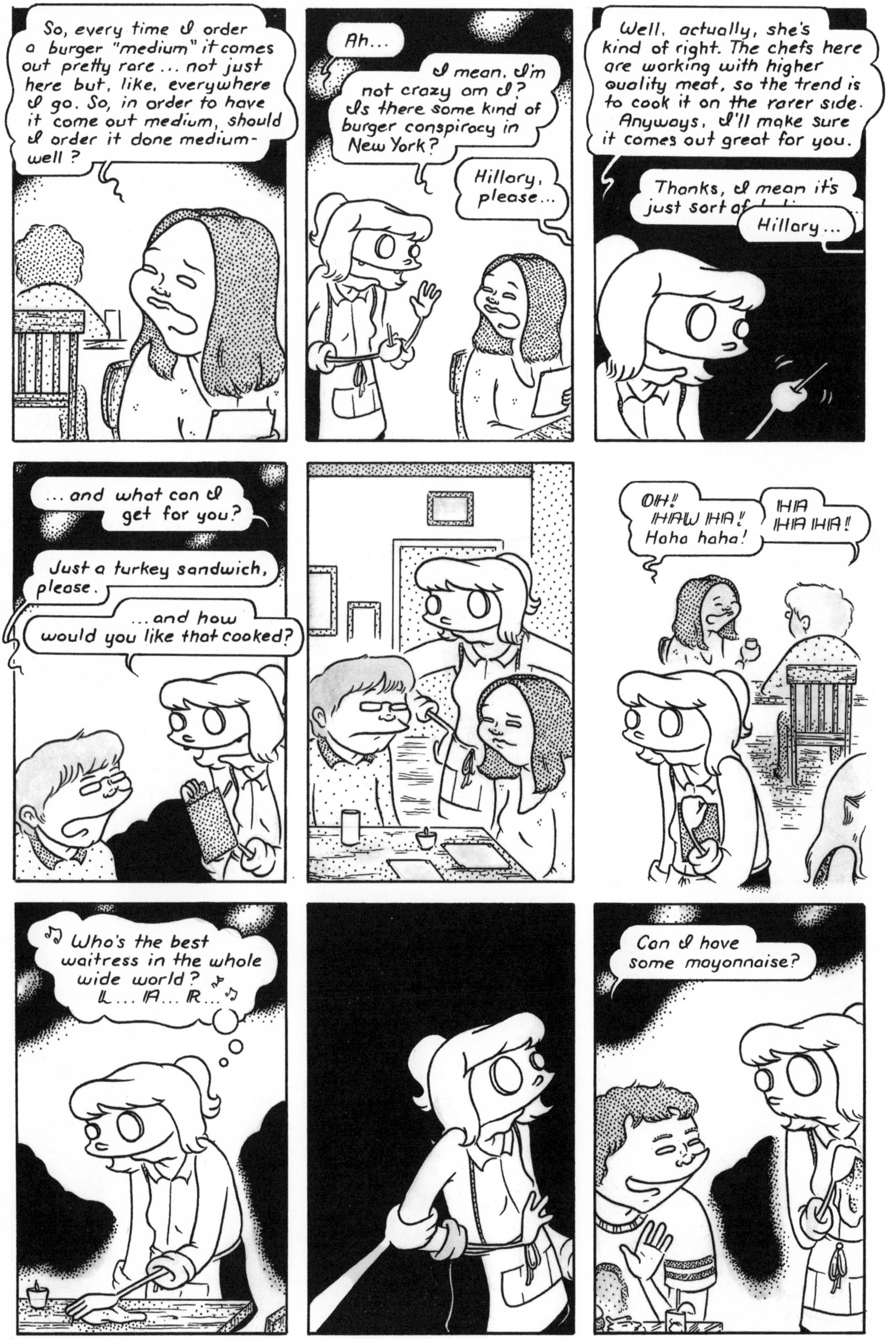
So, every time I order a burger "medium" it comes out pretty rare ... not just here but, like, everywhere I go. So, in order to have it come out medium, should I order it done medium-well?
Ah...
I mean, I'm not crazy am I? Is there some kind of burger conspiracy in New York?
Hillary, please...
Well, actually, she's kind of right. The chefs here are working with higher quality meat, so the trend is to cook it on the rarer side. Anyways, I'll make sure it comes out great for you.
Thanks, I mean it's just sort
Hillary...
... and what can I get for you?
Just a turkey sandwich, please.
... and how would you like that cooked?
OH! HAW HA! Haha haha!
HA HA HA!
Who's the best waitress in the whole wide world? L... A... R...
Can I have some mayonnaise?

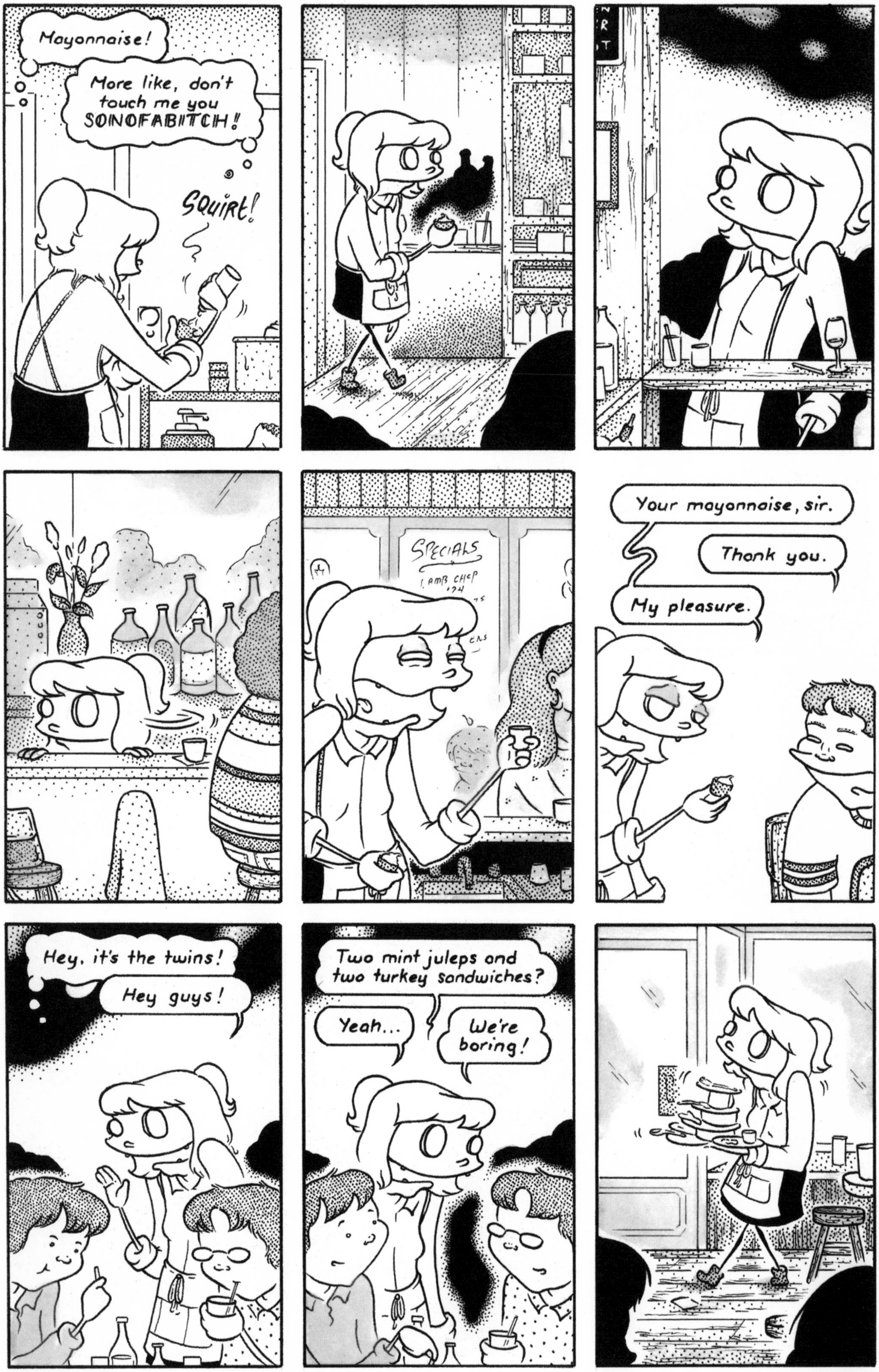
Mayonnaise!
More like, don't touch me you SONOFABITCH!
SQUIRT!
SPECIALS
Your mayonnaise, sir.
Thank you.
My pleasure.
Hey, it's the twins!
Hey guys!
Two mint juleps and two turkey sandwiches?
Yeah...
We're boring!

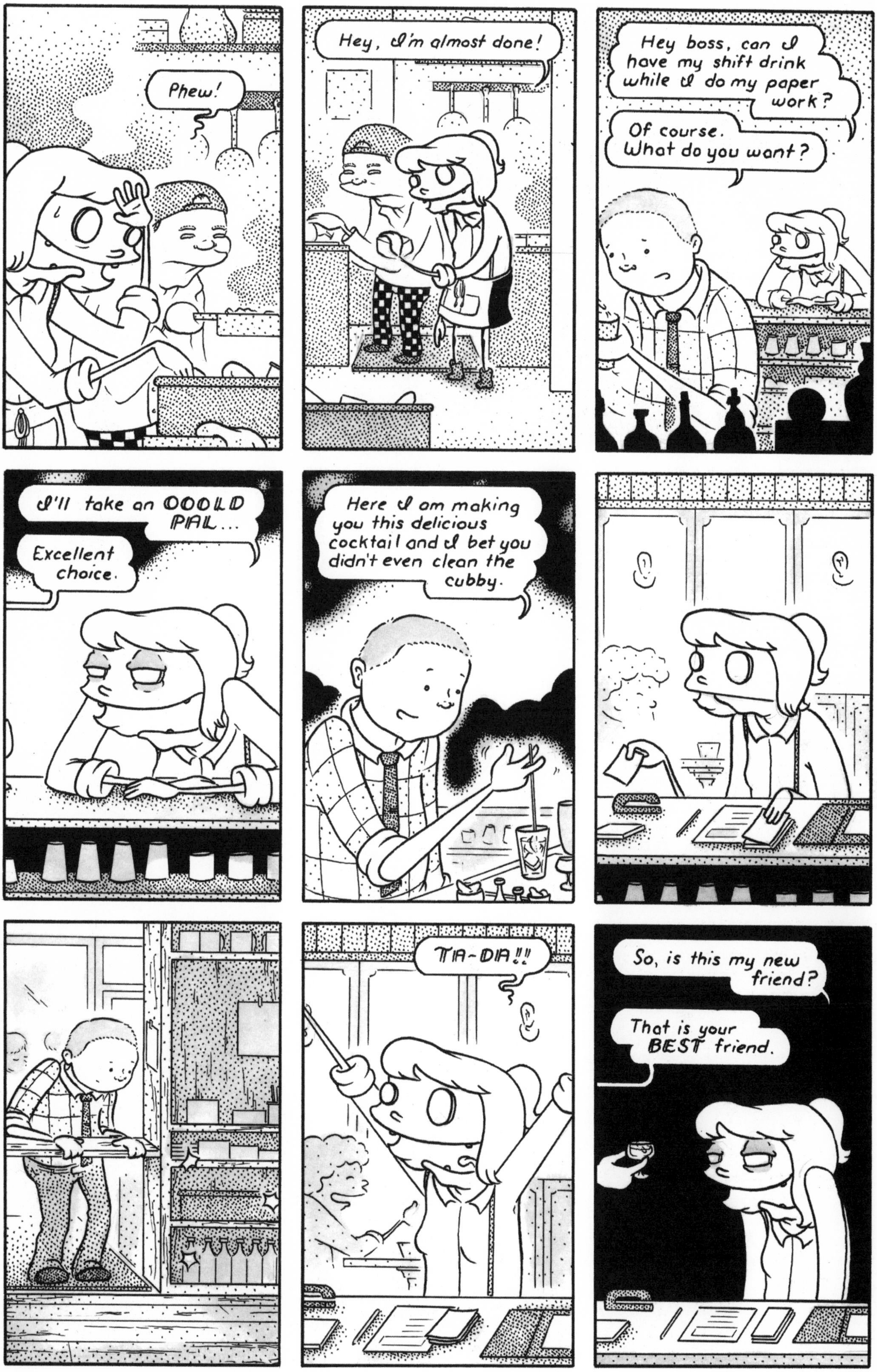
Phew!
Hey, I'm almost done!
Hey boss, can I have my shift drink while I do my paper work?
Of course. What do you want?
I'll take an OOOLD PAL...
Excellent choice.
Here I am making you this delicious cocktail and I bet you didn't even clean the cubby.
TA-DA!!
So, is this my new friend?
That is your BEST friend.

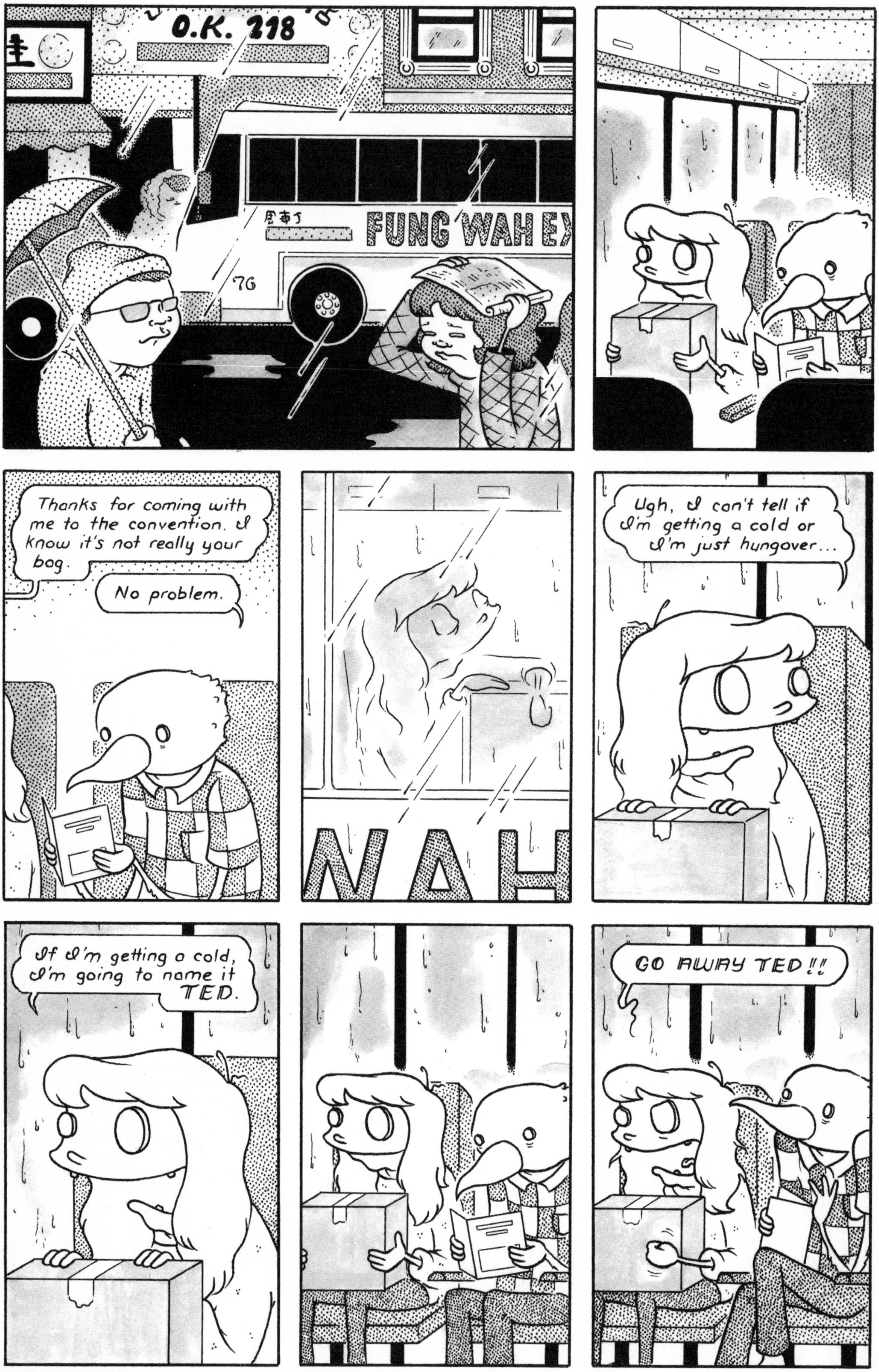
O.K. 218
FUNG WAH EX
76
Thanks for coming with me to the convention. I know it's not really your bag.
No problem.
NAH
Ugh, I can't tell if I'm getting a cold or I'm just hungover...
If I'm getting a cold, I'm going to name it TED.
GO AWAY TED!!

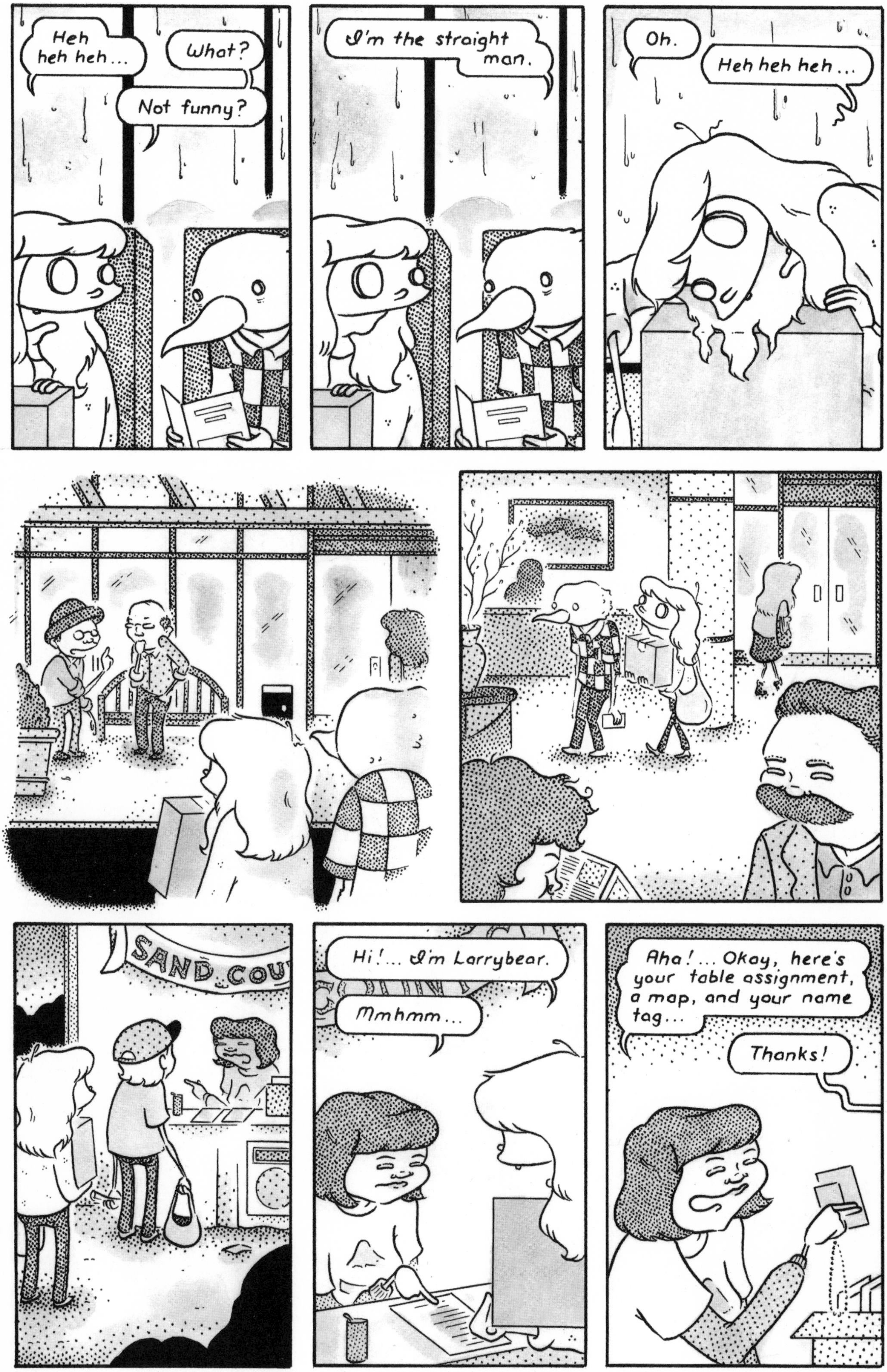

Heh heh heh...
What?
Not funny?
I'm the straight man.
Oh.
Heh heh heh...
SAND COU
Hi!... I'm Larrybear.
Mmhmm...
Aha!... Okay, here's your table assignment, a map, and your name tag...
Thanks!

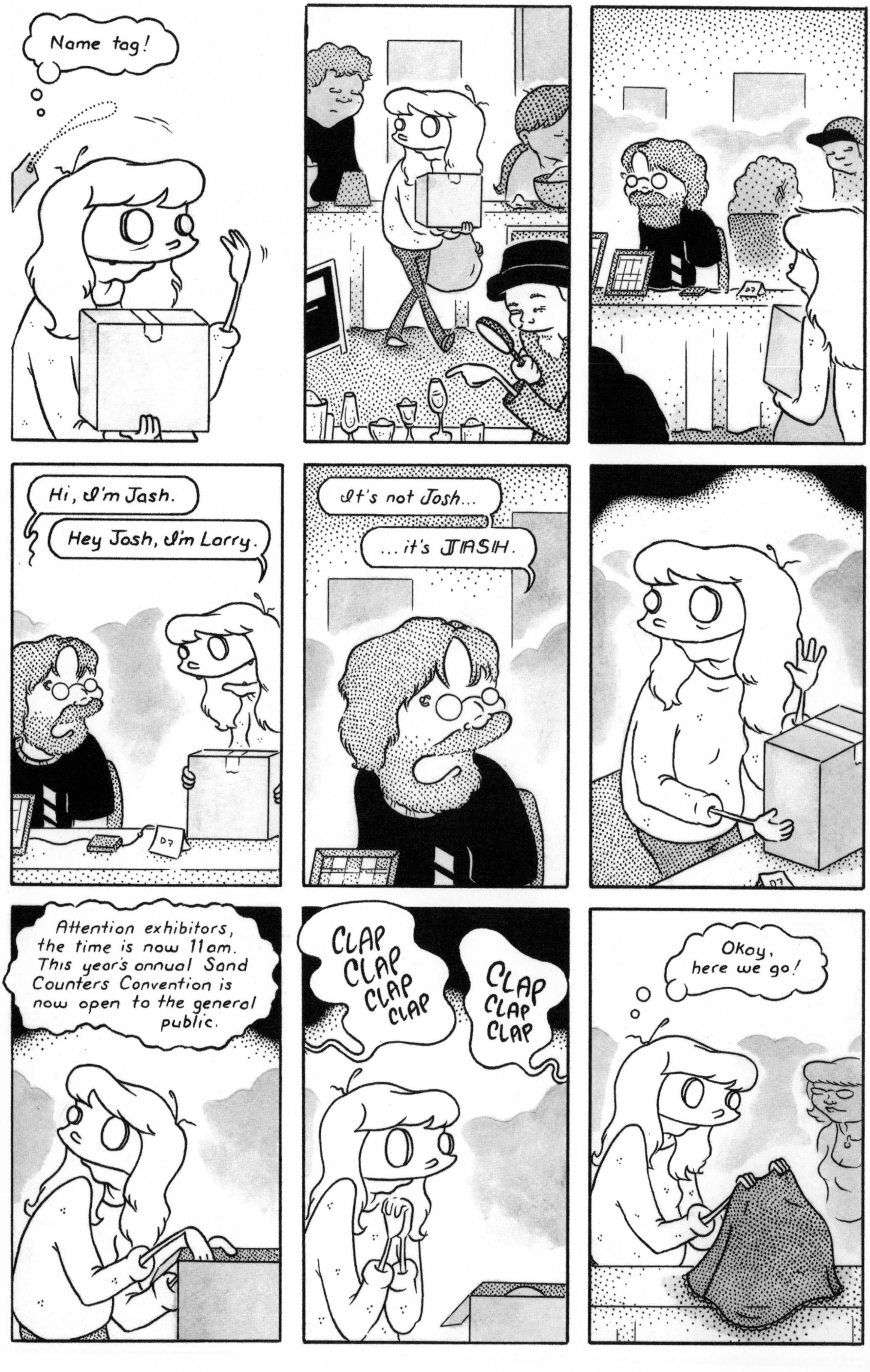
Name tag!
Hi, I'm Jash.
Hey Josh, I'm Larry.
It's not Josh...
... it's JASH.
Attention exhibitors, the time is now 11am. This year's annual Sand Counters Convention is now open to the general public.
CLAP CLAP CLAP CLAP
CLAP CLAP CLAP
Okay, here we go!

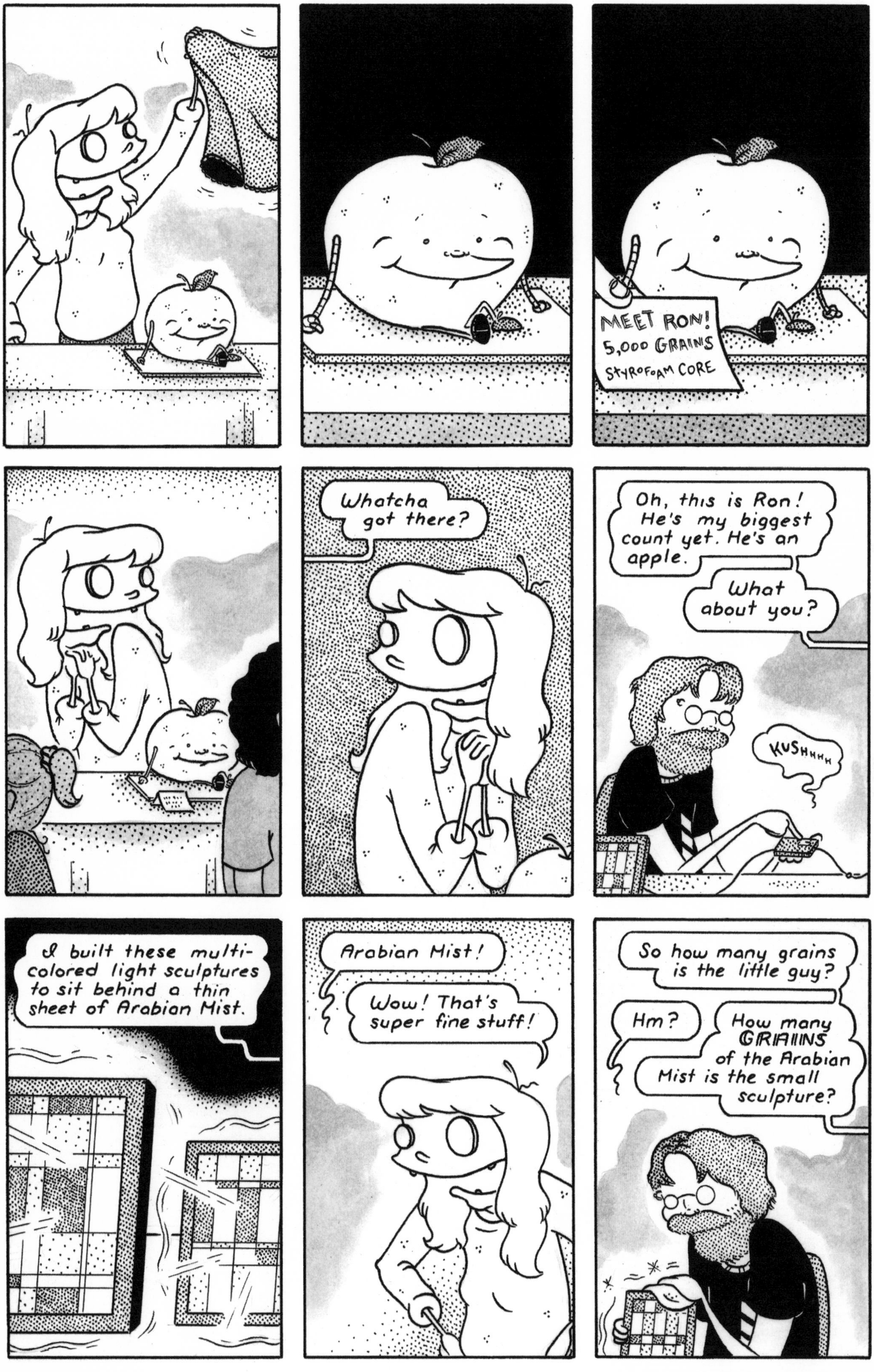

MEET RON!
5,000 GRAINS
STYROFOAM CORE
Whatcha got there?
Oh, this is Ron! He's my biggest count yet. He's an apple.
What about you?
KUSHHHH
I built these multi-colored light sculptures to sit behind a thin sheet of Arabian Mist.
Arabian Mist!
Wow! That's super fine stuff!
So how many grains is the little guy?
Hm?
How many GRAINS of the Arabian Mist is the small sculpture?

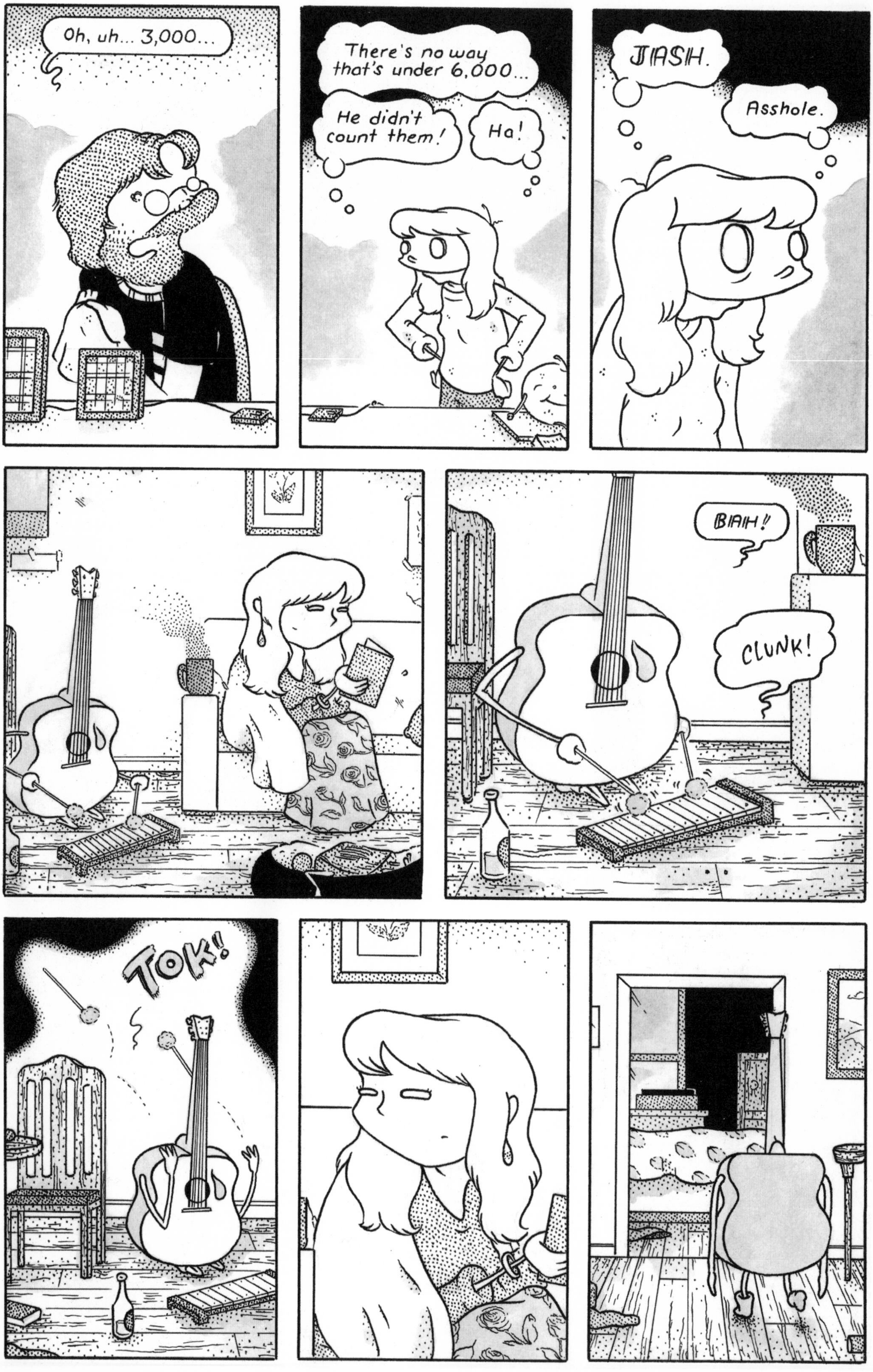

Oh, uh... 3,000...
There's no way that's under 6,000...
He didn't count them!
Ha!
JASH.
Asshole.
BLAH!!
CLUNK!
TOK!

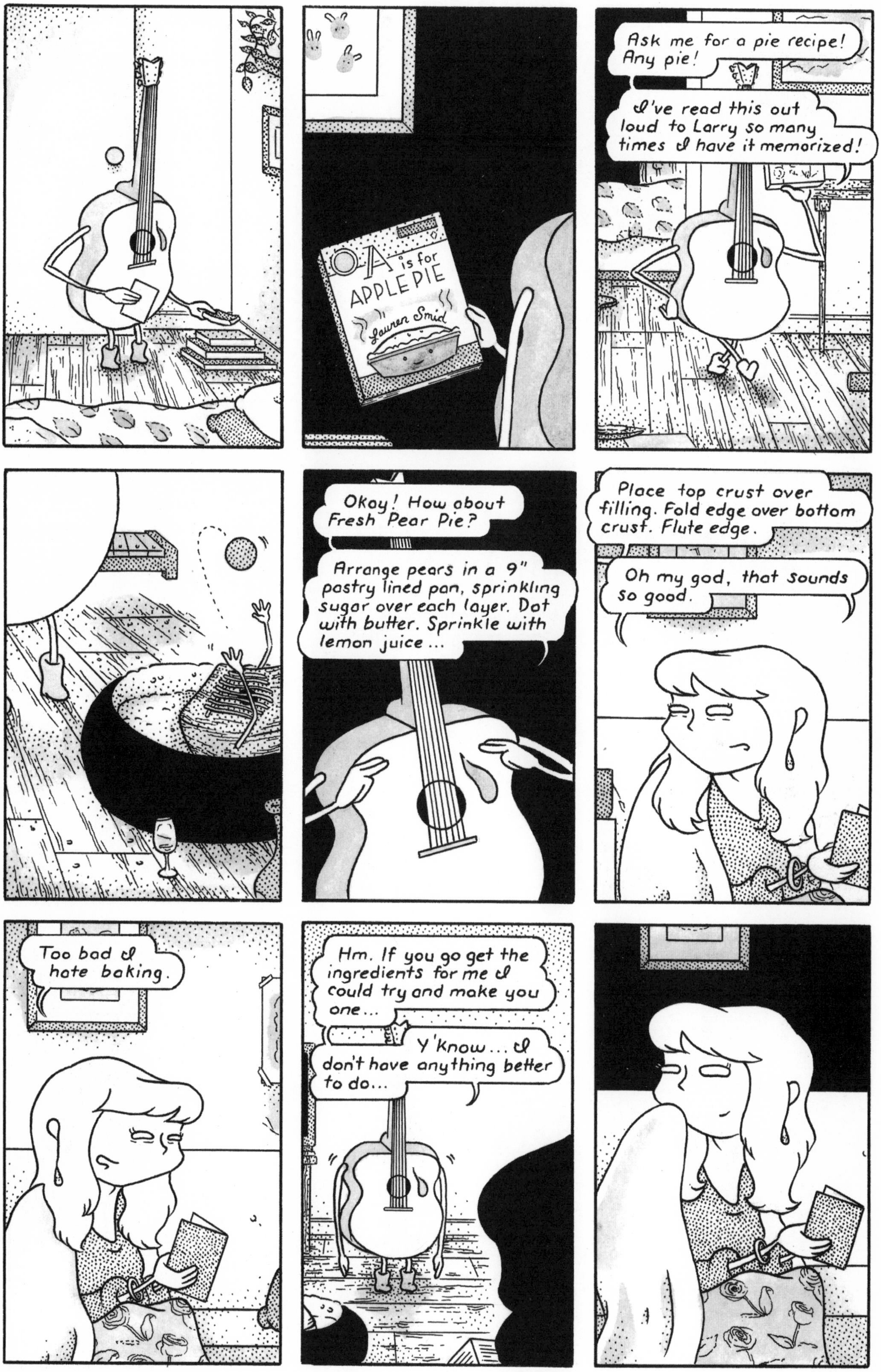
A is for APPLE PIE
Lauren Smid
Ask me for a pie recipe! Any pie!
I've read this out loud to Larry so many times I have it memorized!
Okay! How about Fresh Pear Pie?
Arrange pears in a 9" pastry lined pan, sprinkling sugar over each layer. Dot with butter. Sprinkle with lemon juice...
Place top crust over filling. Fold edge over bottom crust. Flute edge.
Oh my god, that sounds so good.
Too bad I hate baking.
Hm. If you go get the ingredients for me I could try and make you one...
Y'know... I don't have anything better to do...

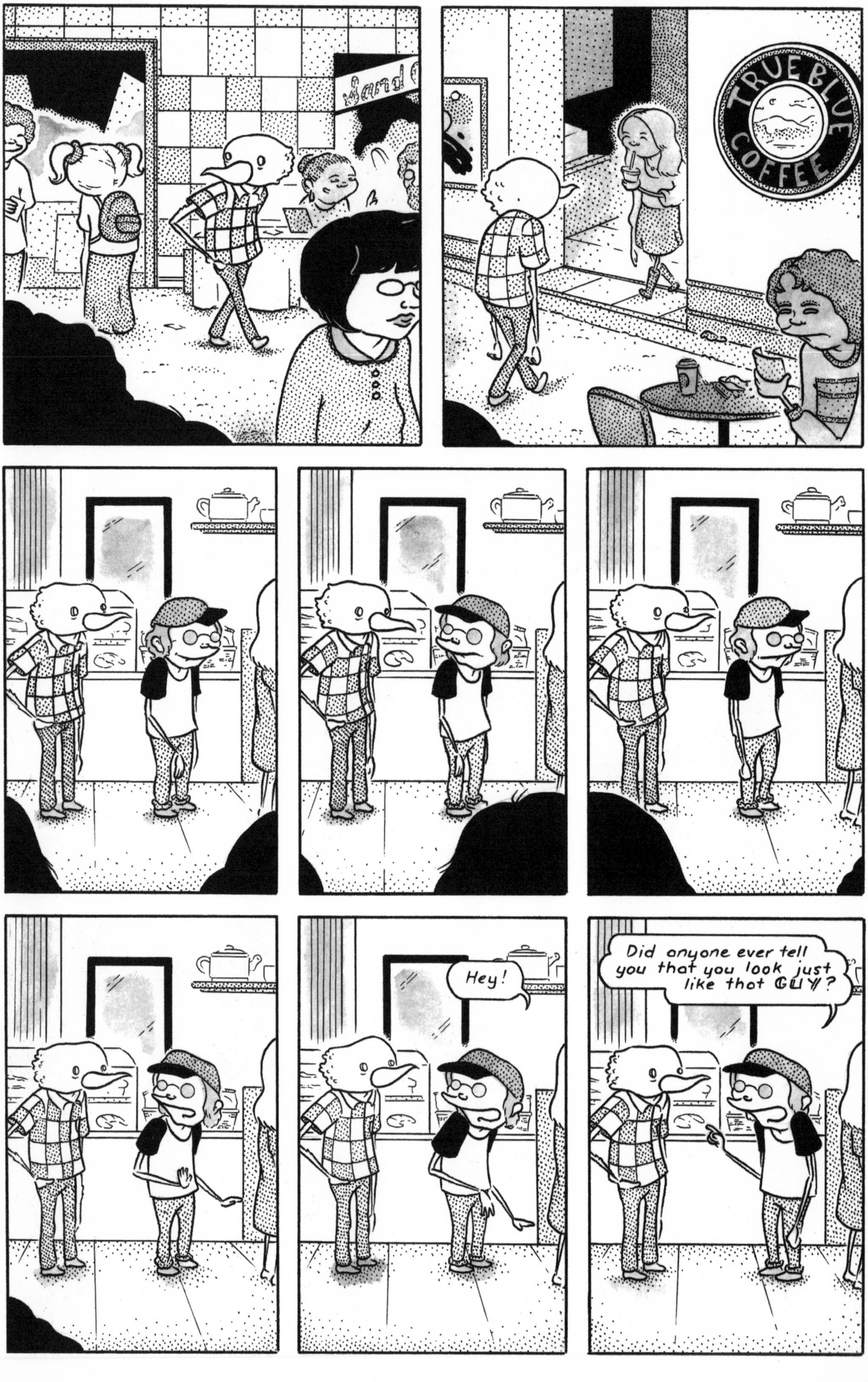
TRUE BLUE COFFEE
Hey!
Did anyone ever tell you that you look just like that GUY?

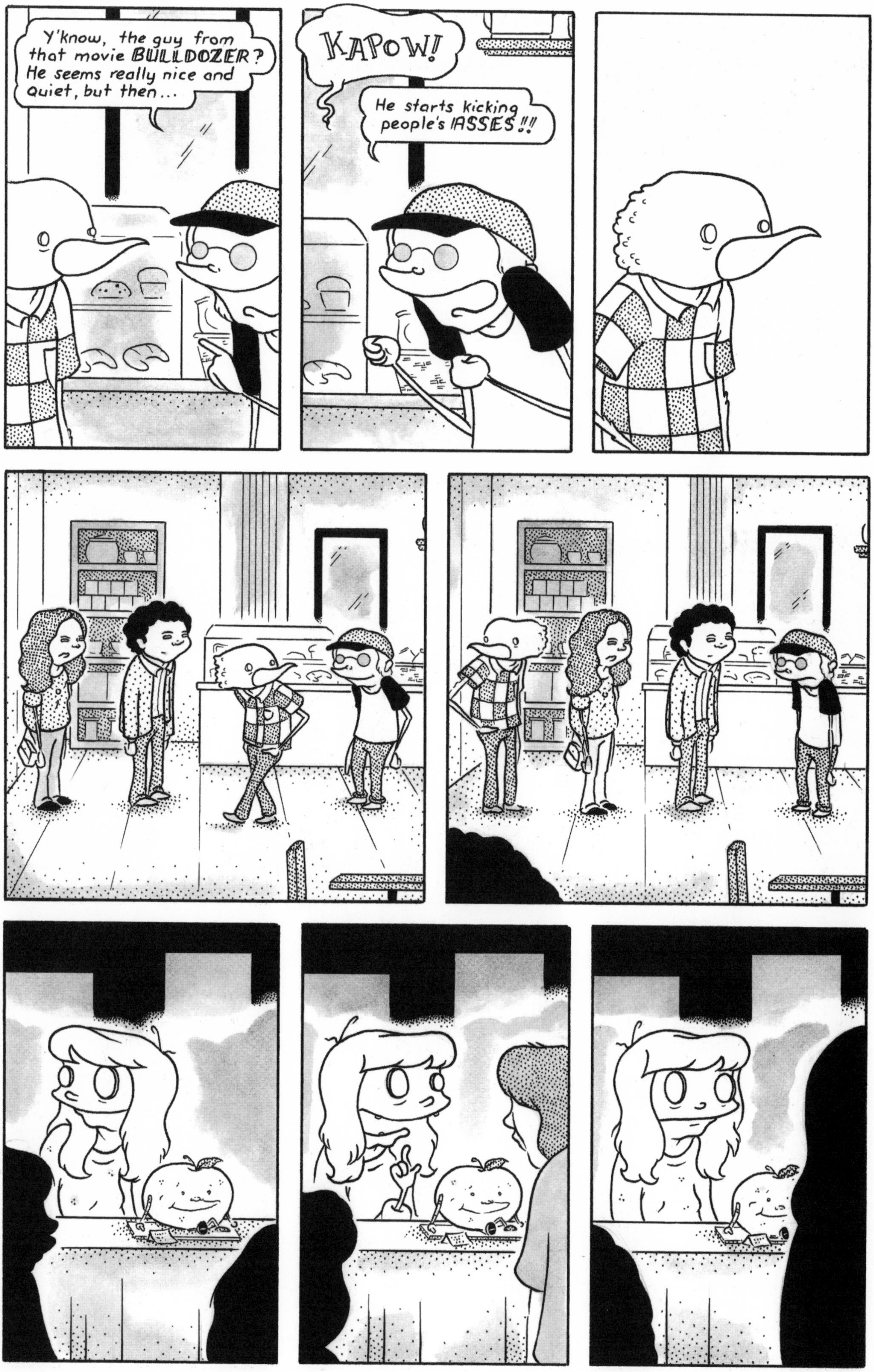
Y'know, the guy from that movie BULLDOZER? He seems really nice and quiet, but then...
KAPOW!
He starts kicking people's ASSES!!

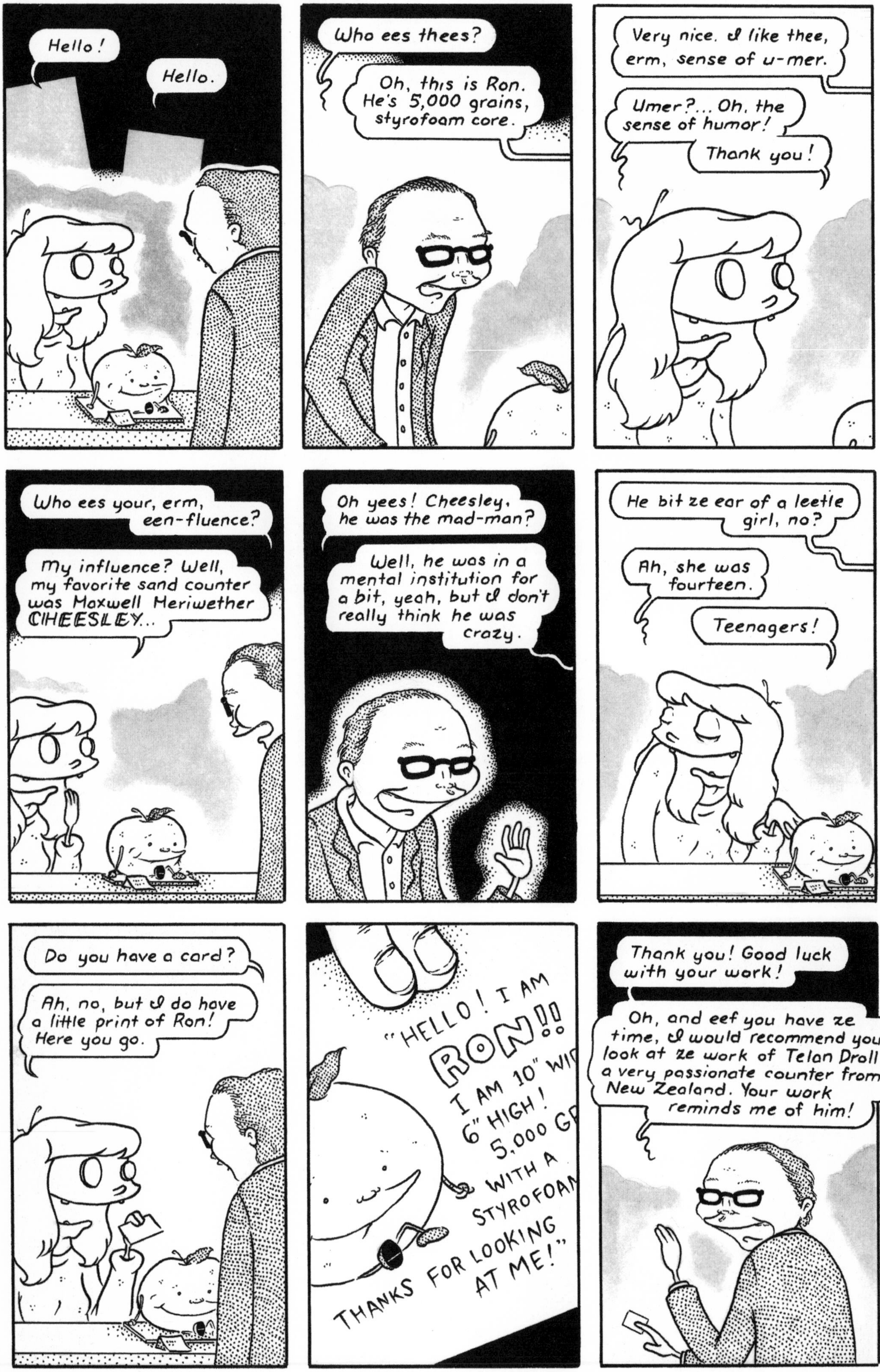
Hello!
Hello.
Who ees thees?
Oh, this is Ron. He's 5,000 grains, styrofoam core.
Very nice. I like thee, erm, sense of u-mer.
Umer?... Oh, the sense of humor!
Thank you!
Who ees your, erm, een-fluence?
My influence? Well, my favorite sand counter was Maxwell Meriwether CHEESLEY...
Oh yees! Cheesley, he was the mad-man?
Well, he was in a mental institution for a bit, yeah, but I don't really think he was crazy.
He bit ze ear of a leetle girl, no?
Ah, she was fourteen.
Teenagers!
Do you have a card?
Ah, no, but I do have a little print of Ron! Here you go.
"HELLO! I AM RON!!
I AM 10" WI
6" HIGH!
5,000 GR
WITH A
STYROFOAM
THANKS FOR LOOKING AT ME!"
Thank you! Good luck with your work!
Oh, and eef you have ze time, I would recommend you look at ze work of Telan Droll, a very passionate counter from New Zealand. Your work reminds me of him!

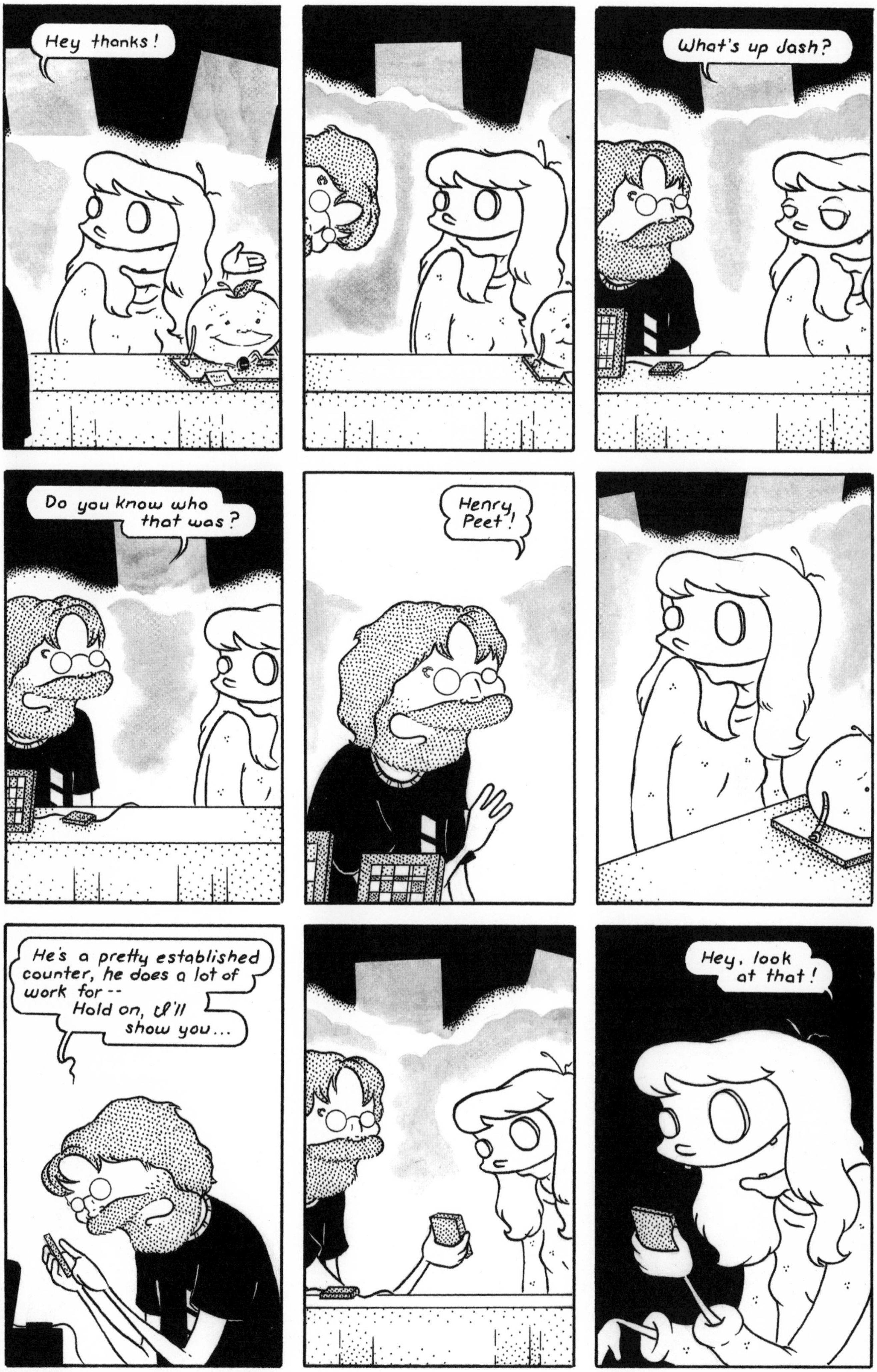

Hey thanks!
What's up Jash?
Do you know who that was?
Henry Peet!
He's a pretty established counter, he does a lot of work for -- Hold on, I'll show you...
Hey, look at that!

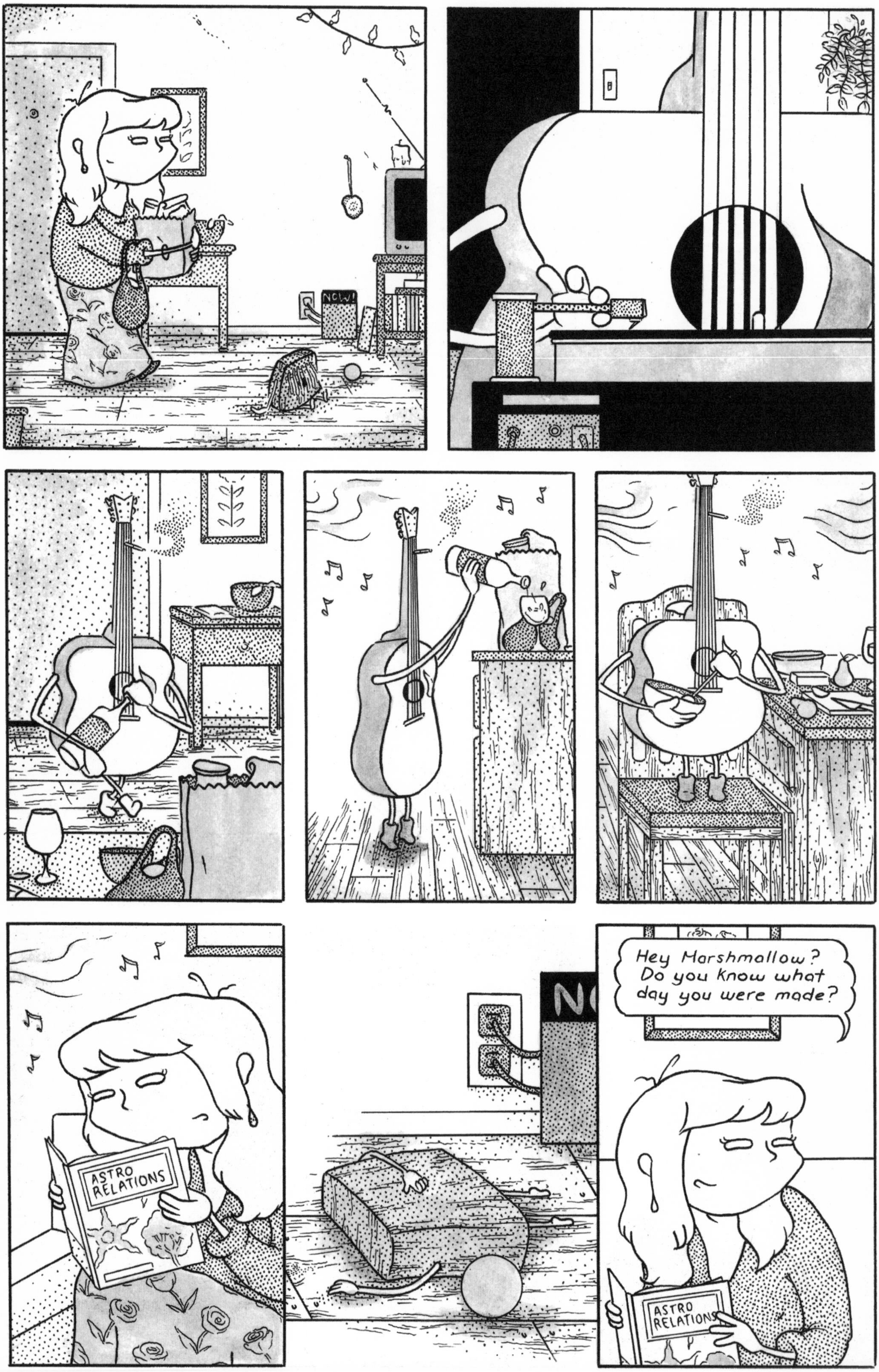
NOW!
ASTRO RELATIONS
Hey Marshmallow? Do you know what day you were made?
ASTRO RELATIONS

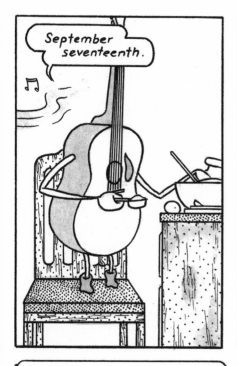

September seventeenth.

Okay, you are a Virgo III, "Week of the Literalist."

Literally. Sarcastic.

You are very nurturing and capable, but you can be judgemental and ruthless...

Dat-da-da... together we... make a good team, are open to new ideas and have a flexible partnership BUT we have to work on being more objective and not let our humor turn hurtful.

What about you and Larry?

"Larry is July fourteenth, "Week of the Persuader." She's enterprising and observant, but she IS prone to excess and could be considered manipulative.

Together we are concerned with life's direction. We instinctively understand where the other is on our life's journey...

Almost psychic, we we are a bit detached, watching eachother from afar... If one of us goes off track...the other will step in to help.

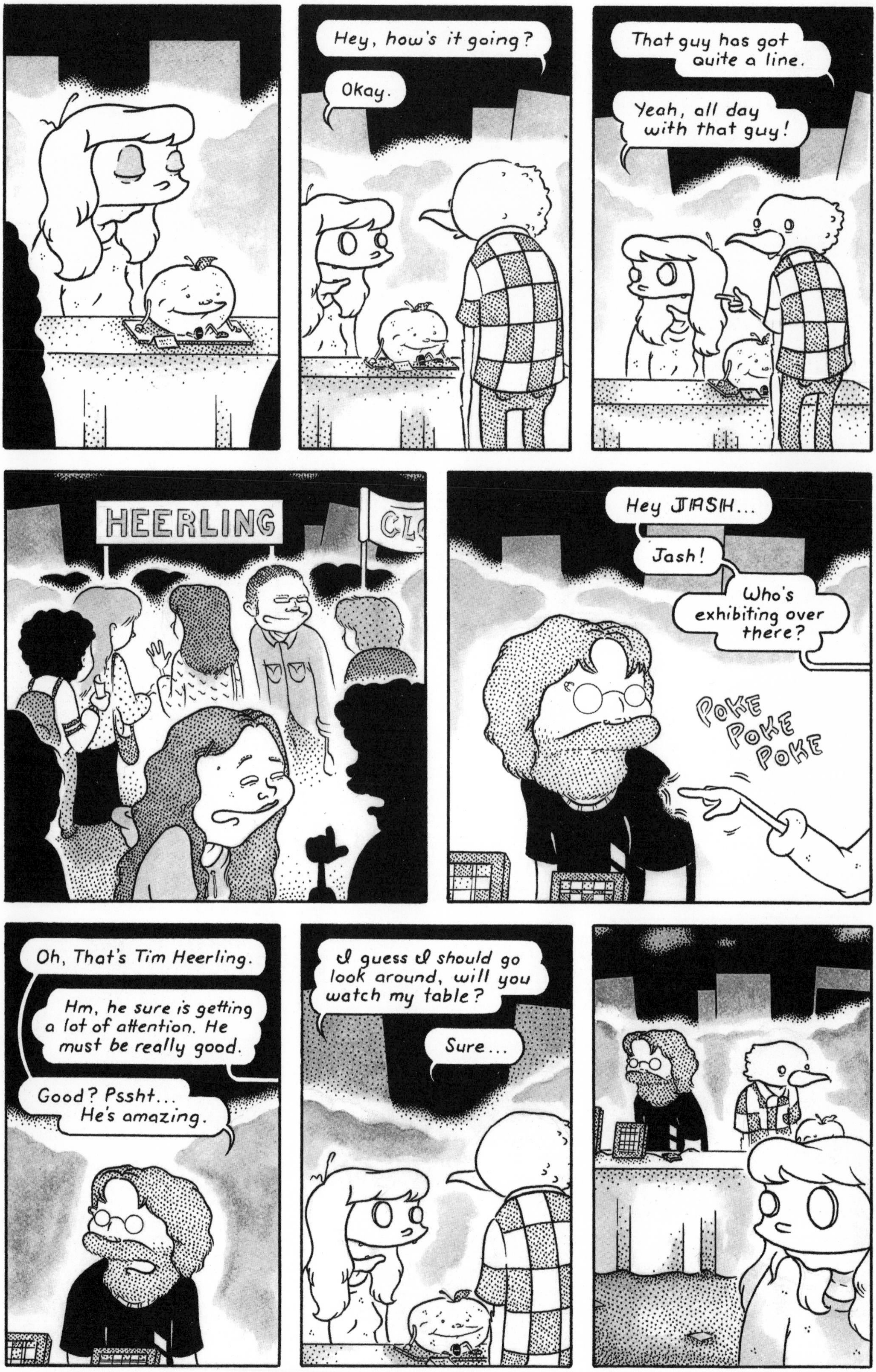
Hey, how's it going?
Okay.
That guy has got quite a line.
Yeah, all day with that guy!
HEERLING
CL
Hey JASH...
Jash!
Who's exhibiting over there?
POKE POKE POKE
Oh, That's Tim Heerling.
Hm, he sure is getting a lot of attention. He must be really good.
Good? Pssht... He's amazing.
I guess I should go look around, will you watch my table?
Sure...

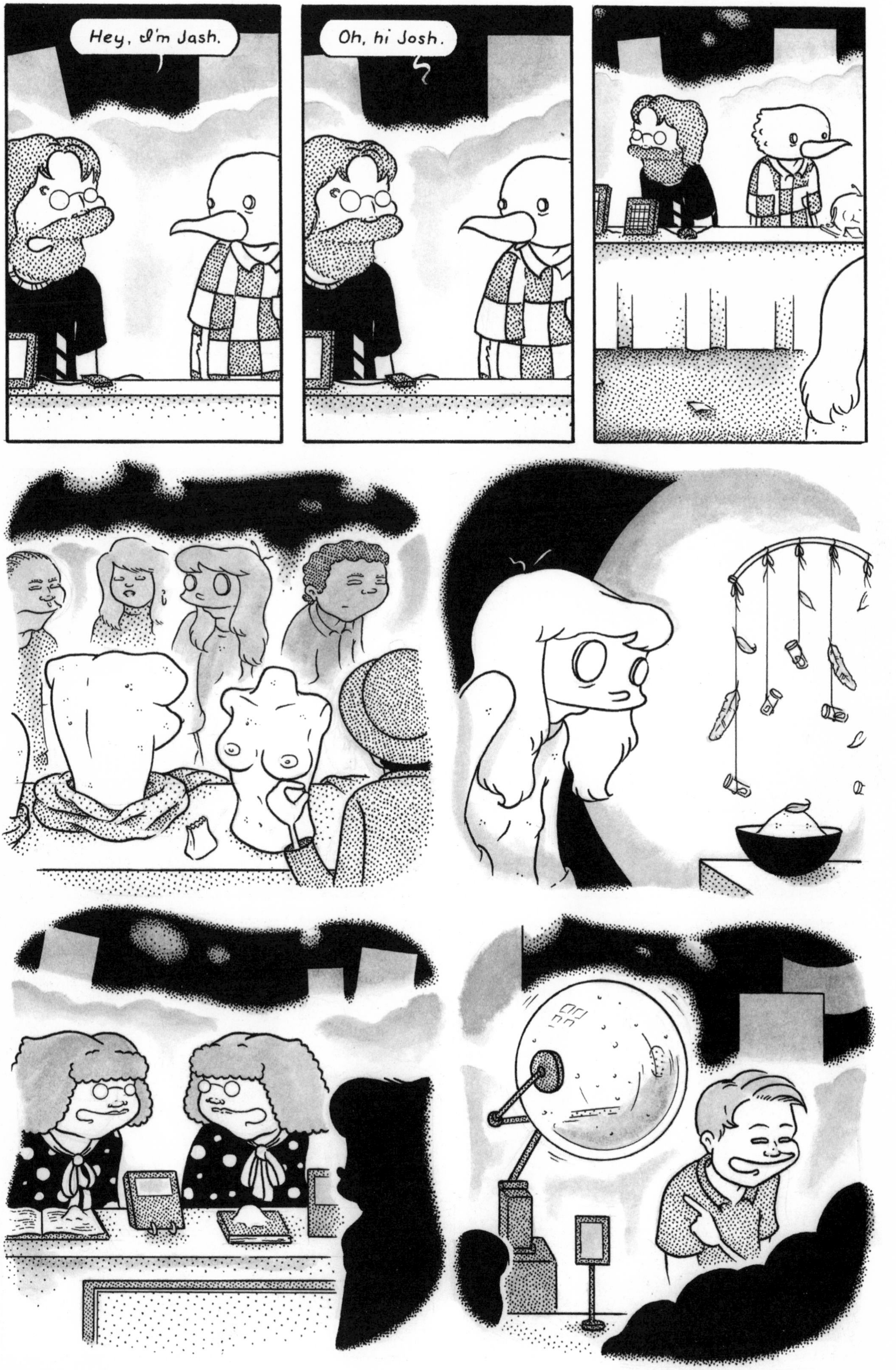
Hey, I'm Jash.
Oh, hi Josh.

HEERLING:
MINIMALIST

DING!

55 60 5
50   10
45   15
40   20
35 25

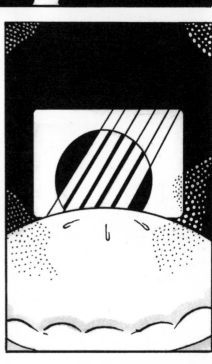

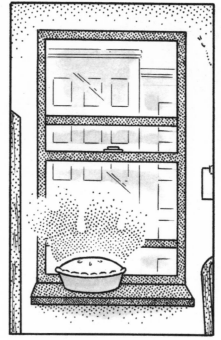

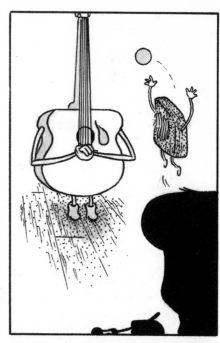

Attention exhibitors,
the time is now 7pm.
This year's annual Sand
Counters Convention has
come to an end. Thank
you for your participation.
We look forward to seeing
you again next year.

CLAP

CLAP

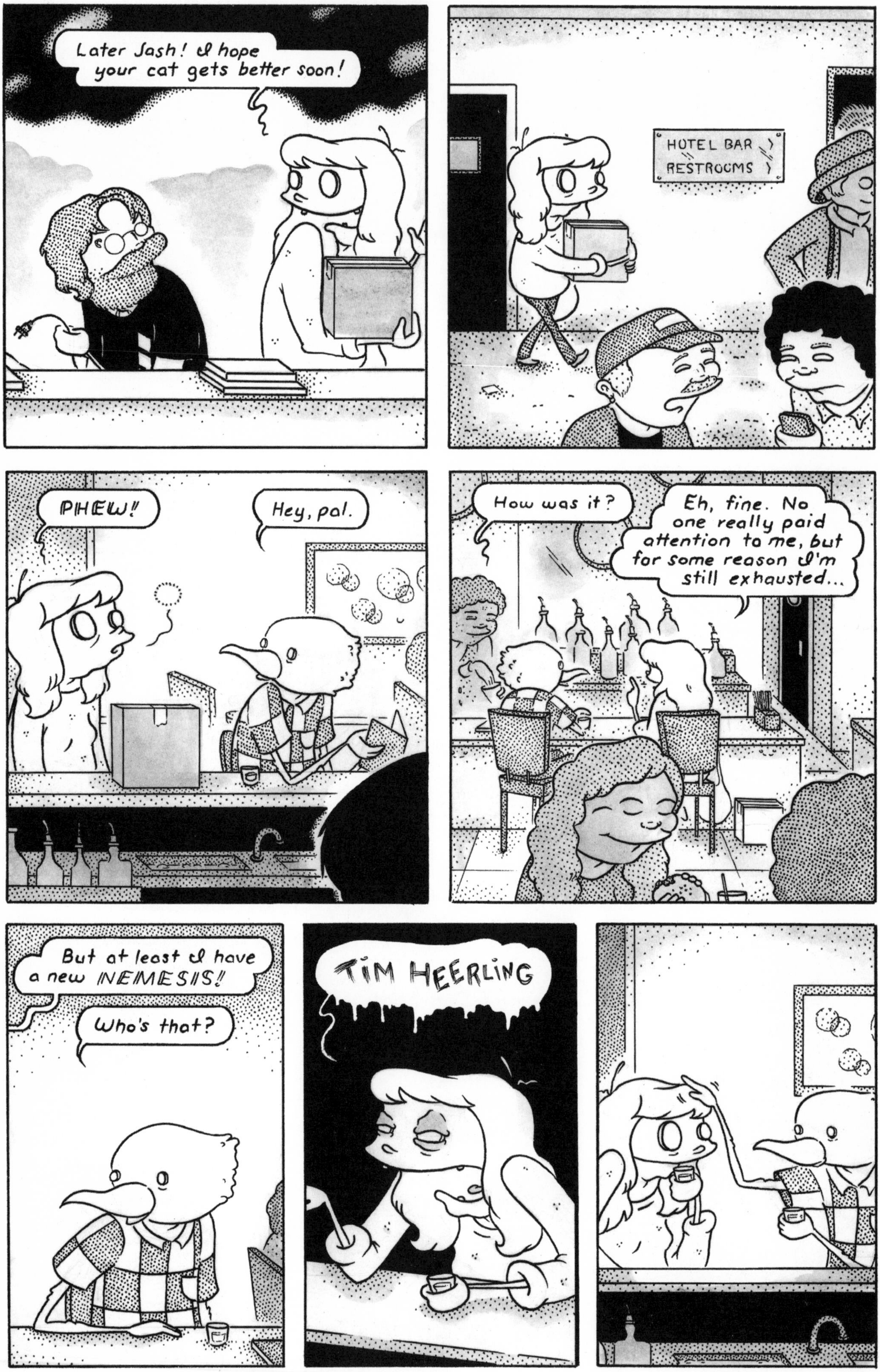
Later Jash! I hope your cat gets better soon!
HOTEL BAR
RESTROOMS
PHEW!
Hey, pal.
How was it?
Eh, fine. No one really paid attention to me, but for some reason I'm still exhausted...
But at least I have a new NEMESIS!
Who's that?
TIM HEERLING

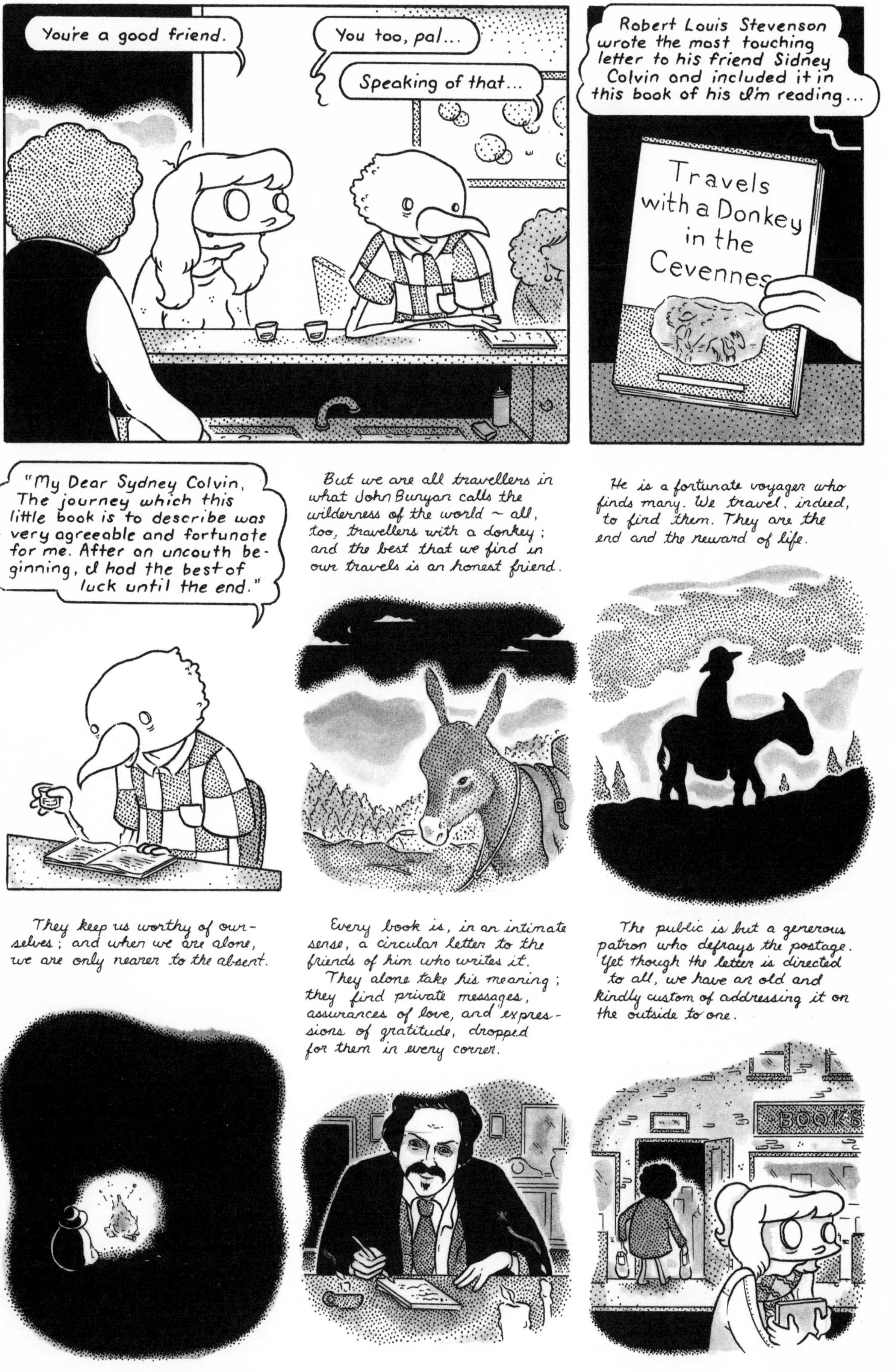

You're a good friend.
You too, pal...
Speaking of that...
Robert Louis Stevenson wrote the most touching letter to his friend Sidney Colvin and included it in this book of his I'm reading...
Travels with a Donkey in the Cevennes
"My Dear Sydney Colvin, The journey which this little book is to describe was very agreeable and fortunate for me. After an uncouth beginning, I had the best of luck until the end."
But we are all travellers in what John Bunyan calls the wilderness of the world ~ all, too, travellers with a donkey; and the best that we find in our travels is an honest friend.
He is a fortunate voyager who finds many. We travel, indeed, to find them. They are the end and the reward of life.
They keep us worthy of ourselves; and when we are alone, we are only nearer to the absent.
Every book is, in an intimate sense, a circular letter to the friends of him who writes it.
They alone take his meaning; they find private messages, assurances of love, and expressions of gratitude, dropped for them in every corner.
The public is but a generous patron who defrays the postage. Yet though the letter is directed to all, we have an old and kindly custom of addressing it on the outside to one.
BOOKS

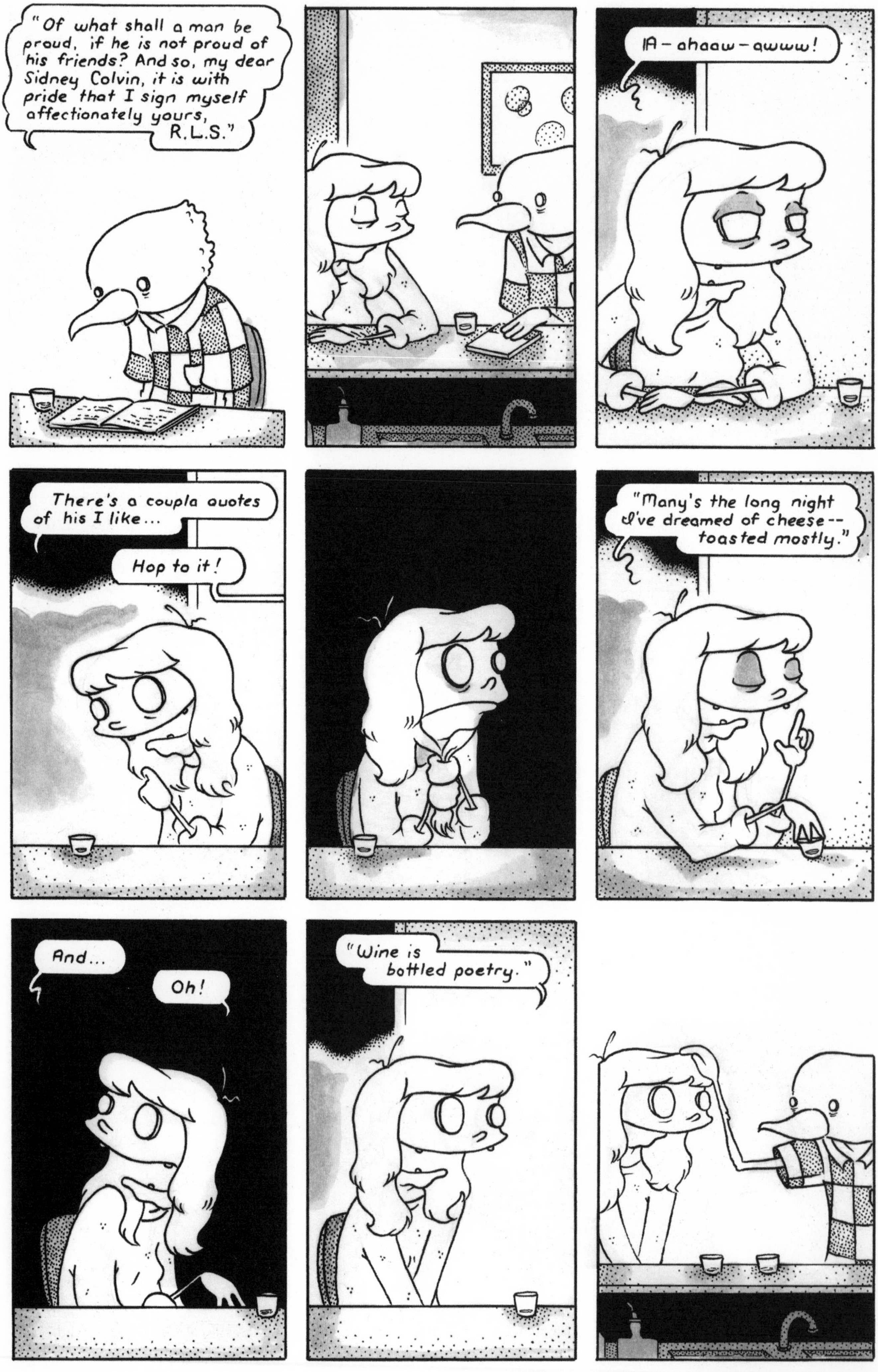
"Of what shall a man be proud, if he is not proud of his friends? And so, my dear Sidney Colvin, it is with pride that I sign myself affectionately yours, R.L.S."
A-ahaaw-awww!
There's a coupla quotes of his I like...
Hop to it!
"Many's the long night I've dreamed of cheese-- toasted mostly."
And...
Oh!
"Wine is bottled poetry."

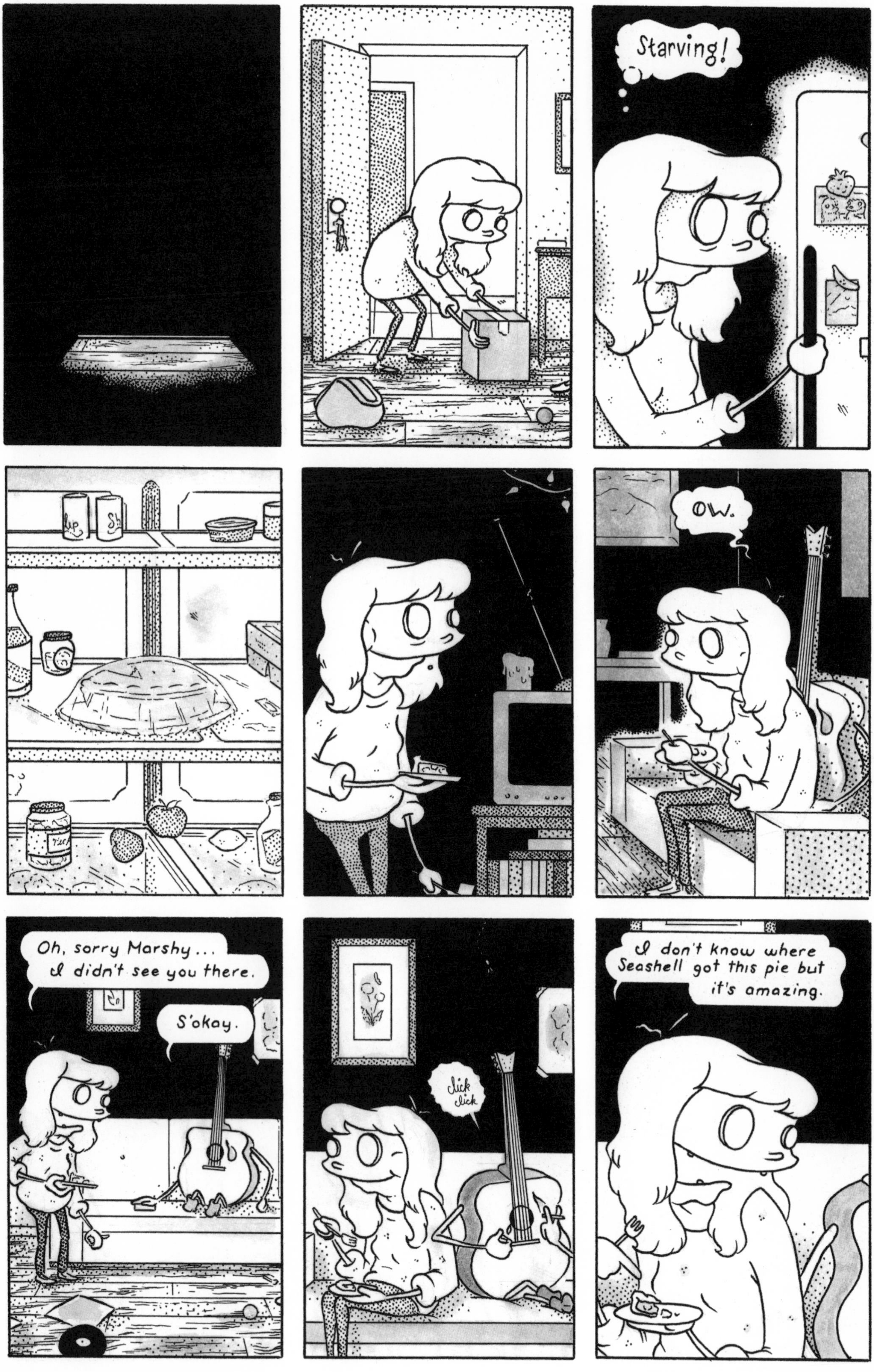
Starving!
OW.
Oh, sorry Marshy... I didn't see you there.
S'okay.
click click
I don't know where Seashell got this pie but it's amazing.

I made that pie.
Ha!
Seriously...
I made that pie.
I think I'm going to make another one tomorrow.
Can you smuggle me into a store this week? I want to look at some pie tins.
Yeah...
Of course.

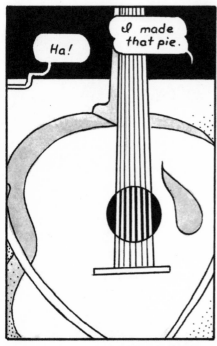

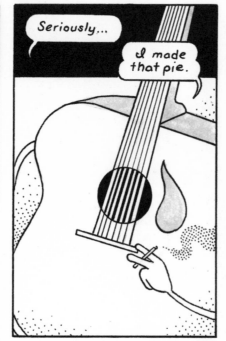

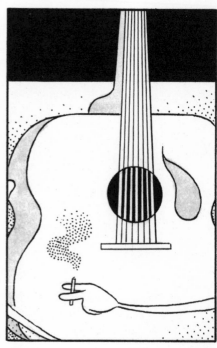

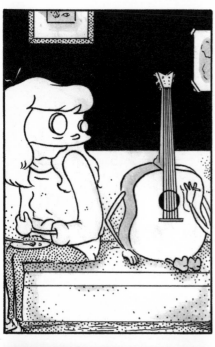

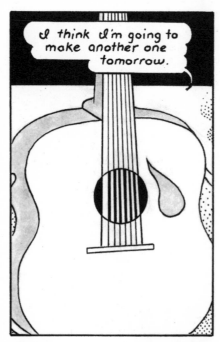

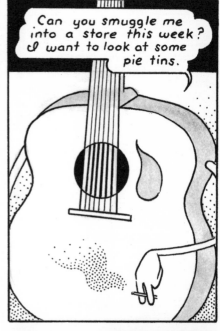

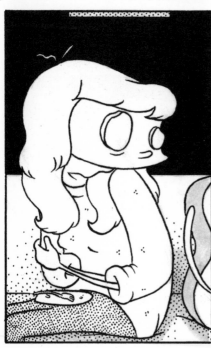

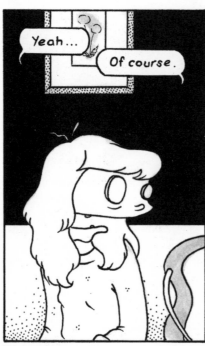

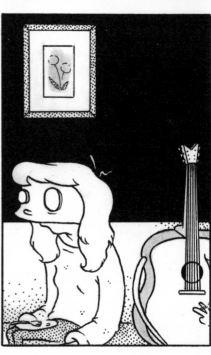

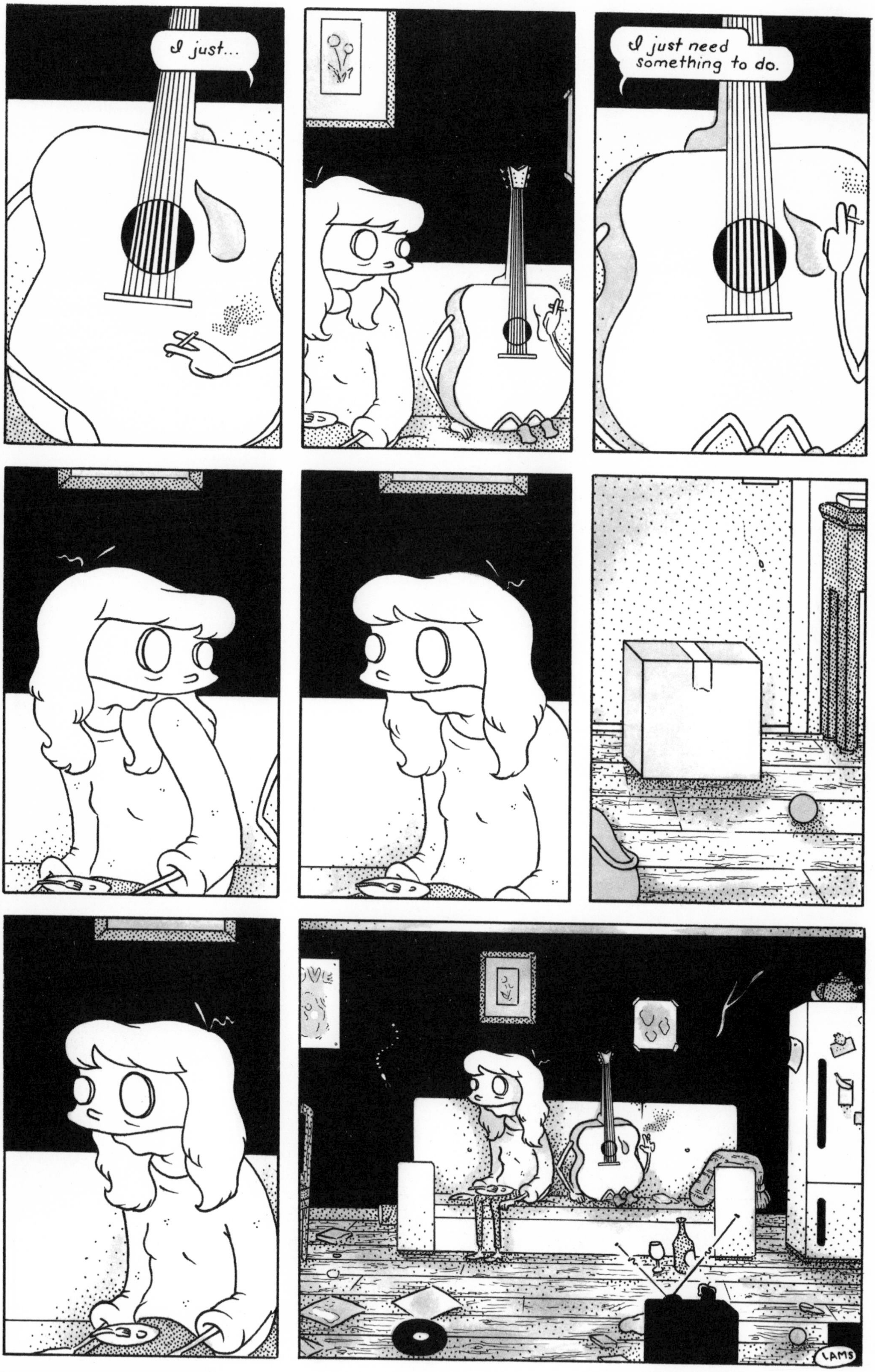
I just...
I just need something to do.
LAMS

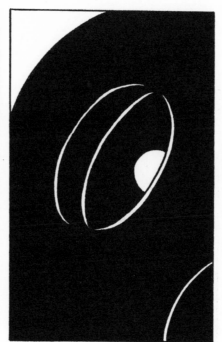

The blue package?

Are you sure this time?

8) 712-5008

tk!

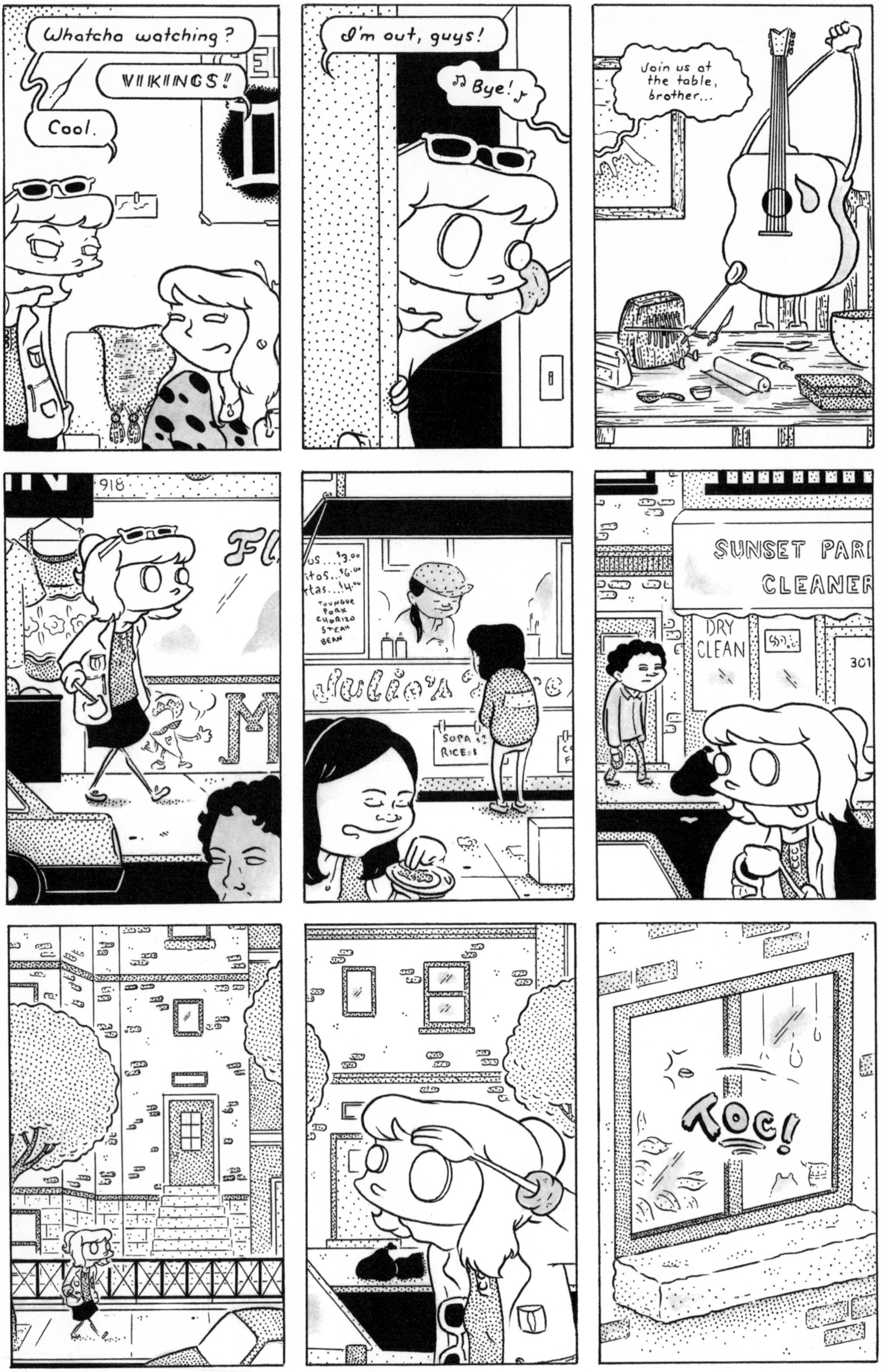
Whatcha watching?
VIKINGS!
Cool.
I'm out, guys!
Bye!
Join us at the table, brother...
918
TOUNGUE
PORK
CHORIZO
STEAK
BEAN
SOPA
RICE
DRY CLEAN
301
TOC!

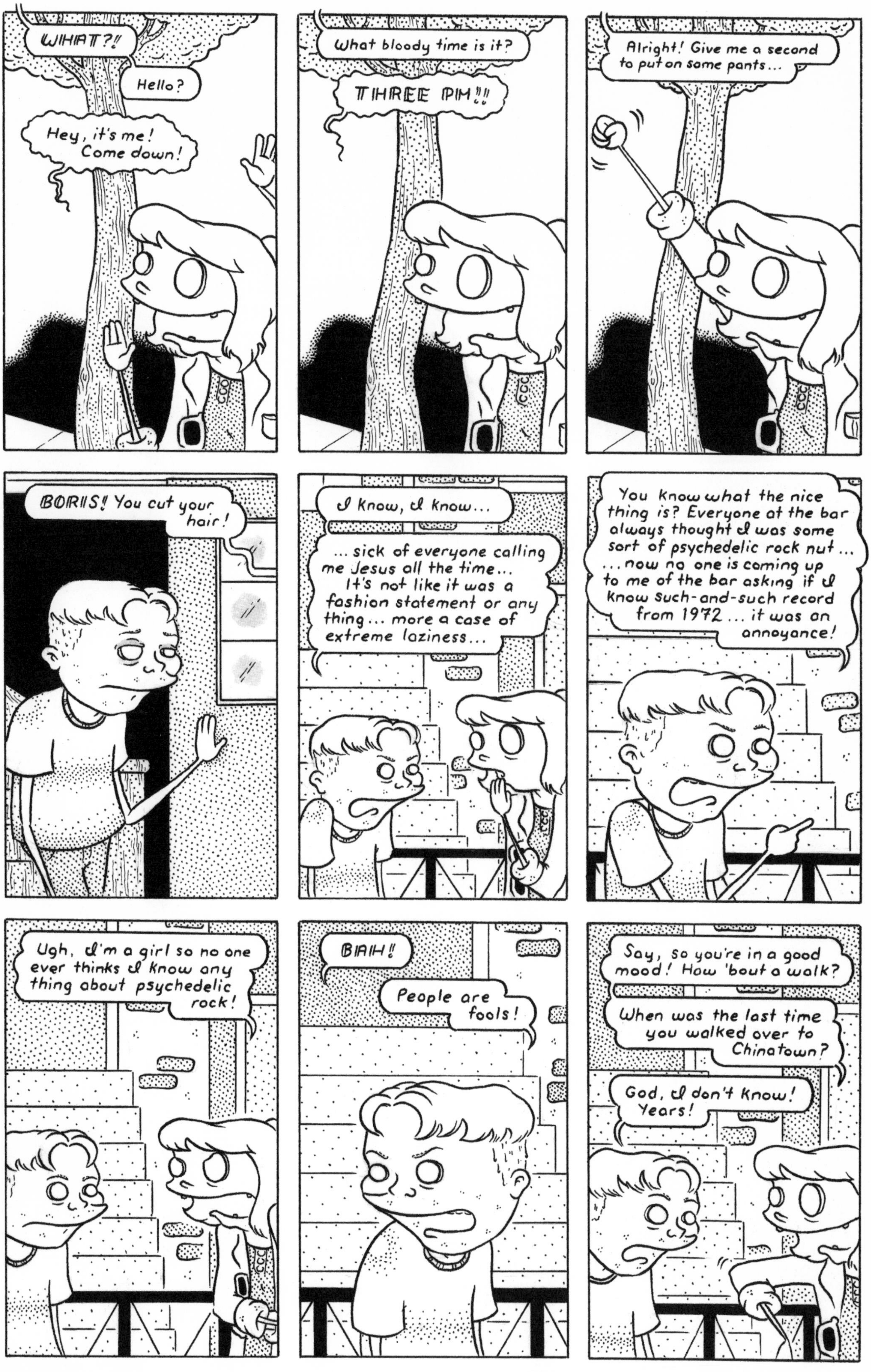
WHAT?!!
Hello?
Hey, it's me! Come down!
What bloody time is it?
THREE PM!!!
Alright! Give me a second to put on some pants...
BORIS! You cut your hair!
I know, I know...
... sick of everyone calling me Jesus all the time... It's not like it was a fashion statement or any thing... more a case of extreme laziness...
You know what the nice thing is? Everyone at the bar always thought I was some sort of psychedelic rock nut ... ... now no one is coming up to me at the bar asking if I know such-and-such record from 1972 ... it was an annoyance!
Ugh, I'm a girl so no one ever thinks I know any thing about psychedelic rock!
BAH!!
People are fools!
Say, so you're in a good mood! How 'bout a walk?
When was the last time you walked over to Chinatown?
God, I don't know! Years!

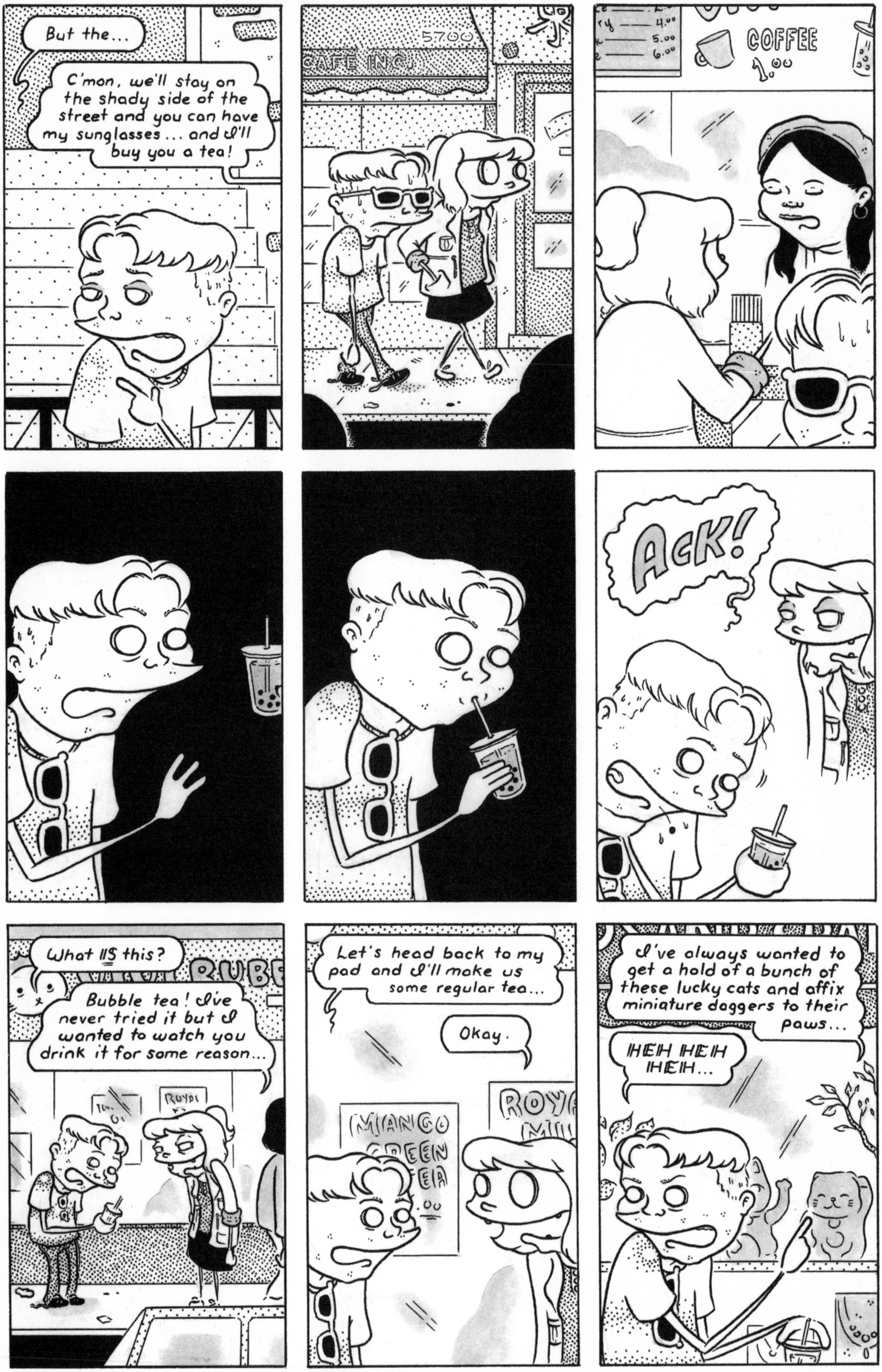
But the...
C'mon, we'll stay on the shady side of the street and you can have my sunglasses... and I'll buy you a tea!
CAFE INC.
5700
COFFEE 1.00
ACK!
What IS this?
Bubble tea! I've never tried it but I wanted to watch you drink it for some reason...
Let's head back to my pad and I'll make us some regular tea...
Okay.
MANGO GREEN TEA
I've always wanted to get a hold of a bunch of these lucky cats and affix miniature daggers to their paws...
HEH HEH HEH...

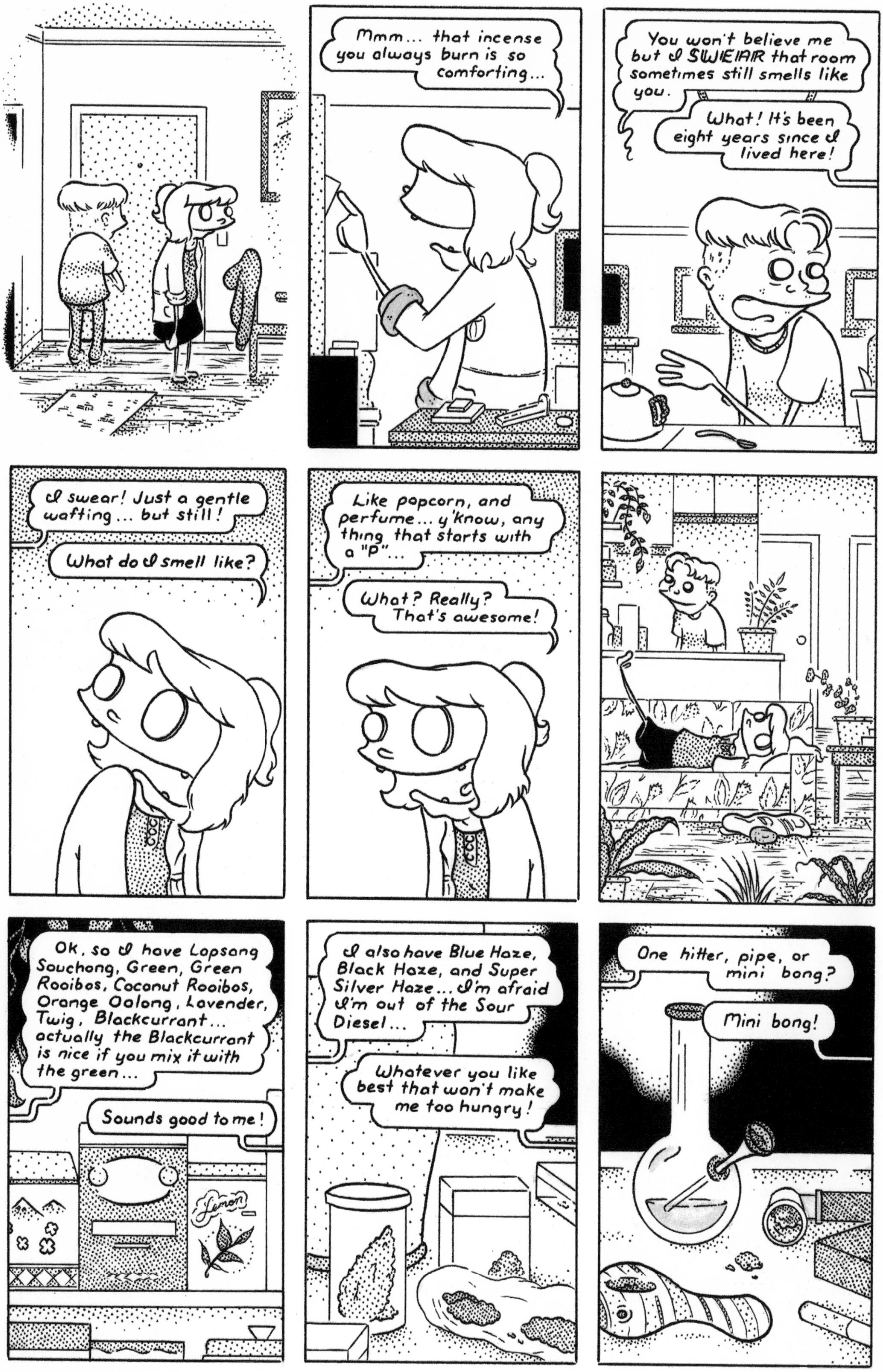
Mmm... that incense you always burn is so comforting...
You won't believe me but I SWEAR that room sometimes still smells like you.
What! It's been eight years since I lived here!
I swear! Just a gentle wafting... but still!
What do I smell like?
Like popcorn, and perfume... y'know, any thing that starts with a "P"...
What? Really? That's awesome!
Ok, so I have Lapsang Souchong, Green, Green Rooibos, Coconut Rooibos, Orange Oolong, Lavender, Twig, Blackcurrant... actually the Blackcurrant is nice if you mix it with the green...
Sounds good to me!
Lemon
I also have Blue Haze, Black Haze, and Super Silver Haze... I'm afraid I'm out of the Sour Diesel...
Whatever you like best that won't make me too hungry!
One hitter, pipe, or mini bong?
Mini bong!

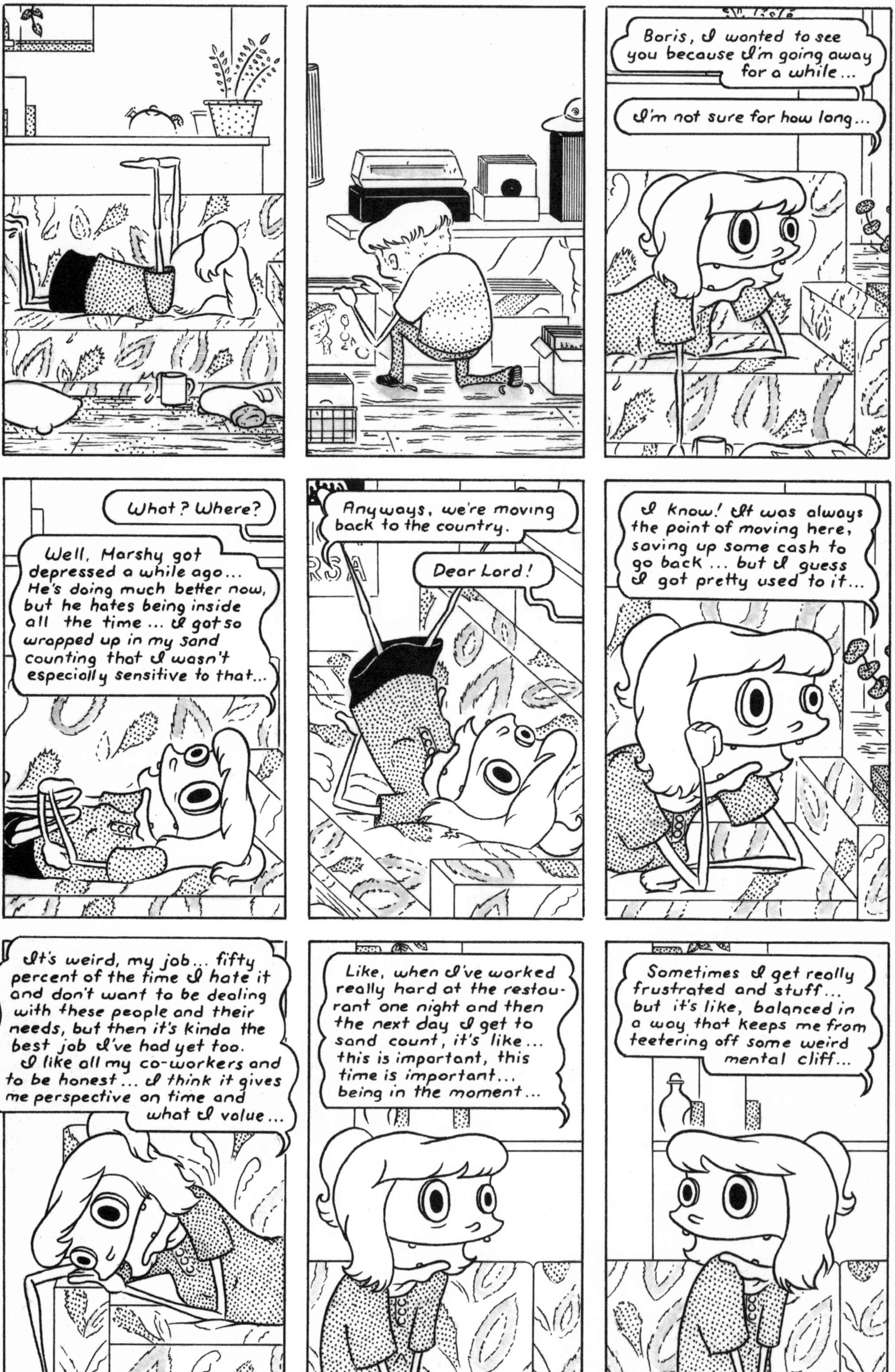
Boris, I wanted to see you because I'm going away for a while...
I'm not sure for how long...
What? Where?
Well, Marshy got depressed a while ago... He's doing much better now, but he hates being inside all the time... I got so wrapped up in my sand counting that I wasn't especially sensitive to that...
Anyways, we're moving back to the country.
Dear Lord!
I know! It was always the point of moving here, saving up some cash to go back... but I guess I got pretty used to it...
It's weird, my job... fifty percent of the time I hate it and don't want to be dealing with these people and their needs, but then it's kinda the best job I've had yet too. I like all my co-workers and to be honest... I think it gives me perspective on time and what I value...
Like, when I've worked really hard at the restaurant one night and then the next day I get to sand count, it's like... this is important, this time is important... being in the moment...
Sometimes I get really frustrated and stuff... but it's like, balanced in a way that keeps me from teetering off some weird mental cliff...

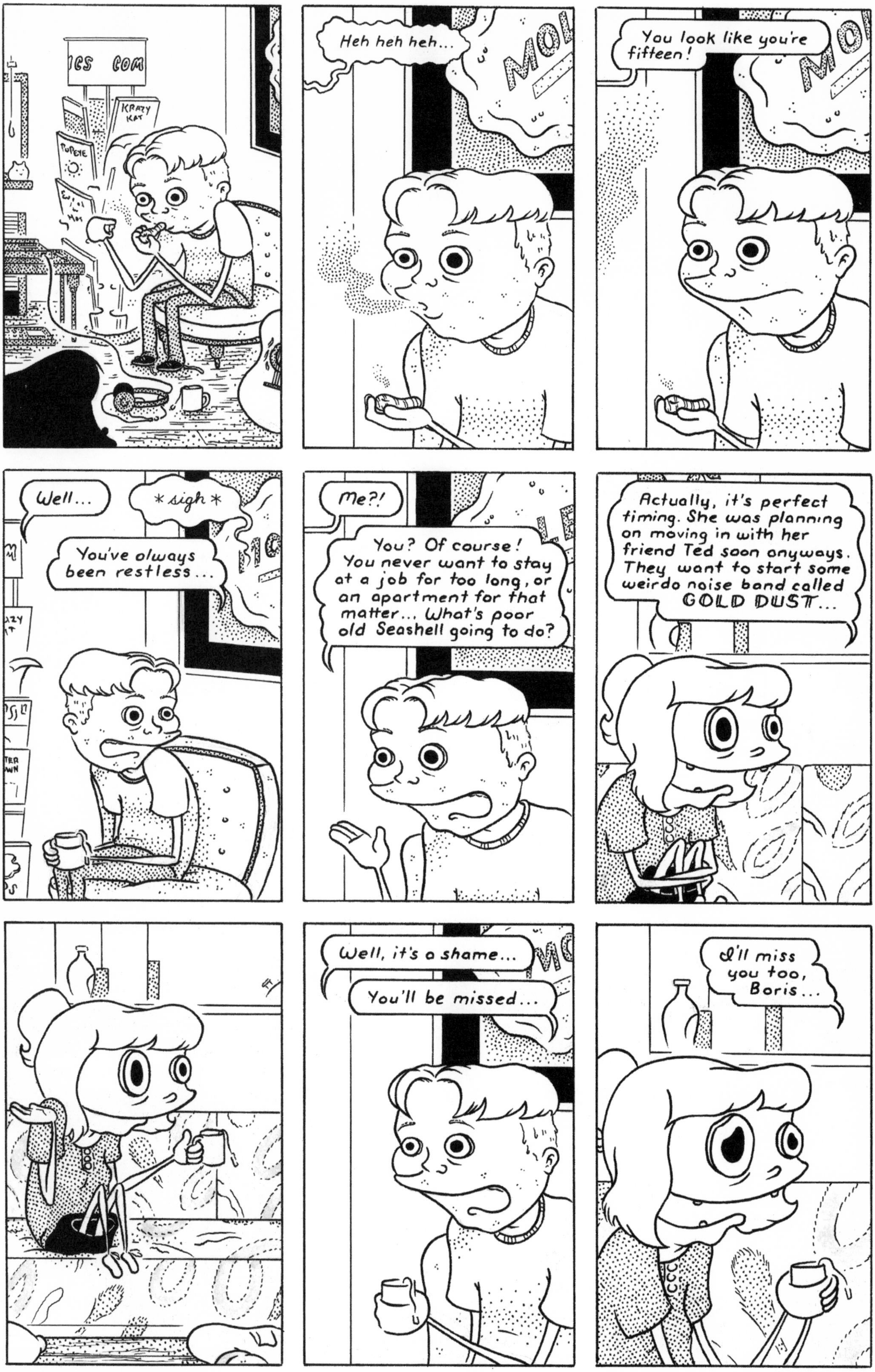
ICS COM
KRAZY KAT
POPEYE
Heh heh heh...
You look like you're fifteen!
Well...
sigh
You've always been restless...
Me?!
You? Of course! You never want to stay at a job for too long, or an apartment for that matter... What's poor old Seashell going to do?
Actually, it's perfect timing. She was planning on moving in with her friend Ted soon anyways. They want to start some weirdo noise band called GOLD DUST...
Well, it's a shame...
You'll be missed...
I'll miss you too, Boris...

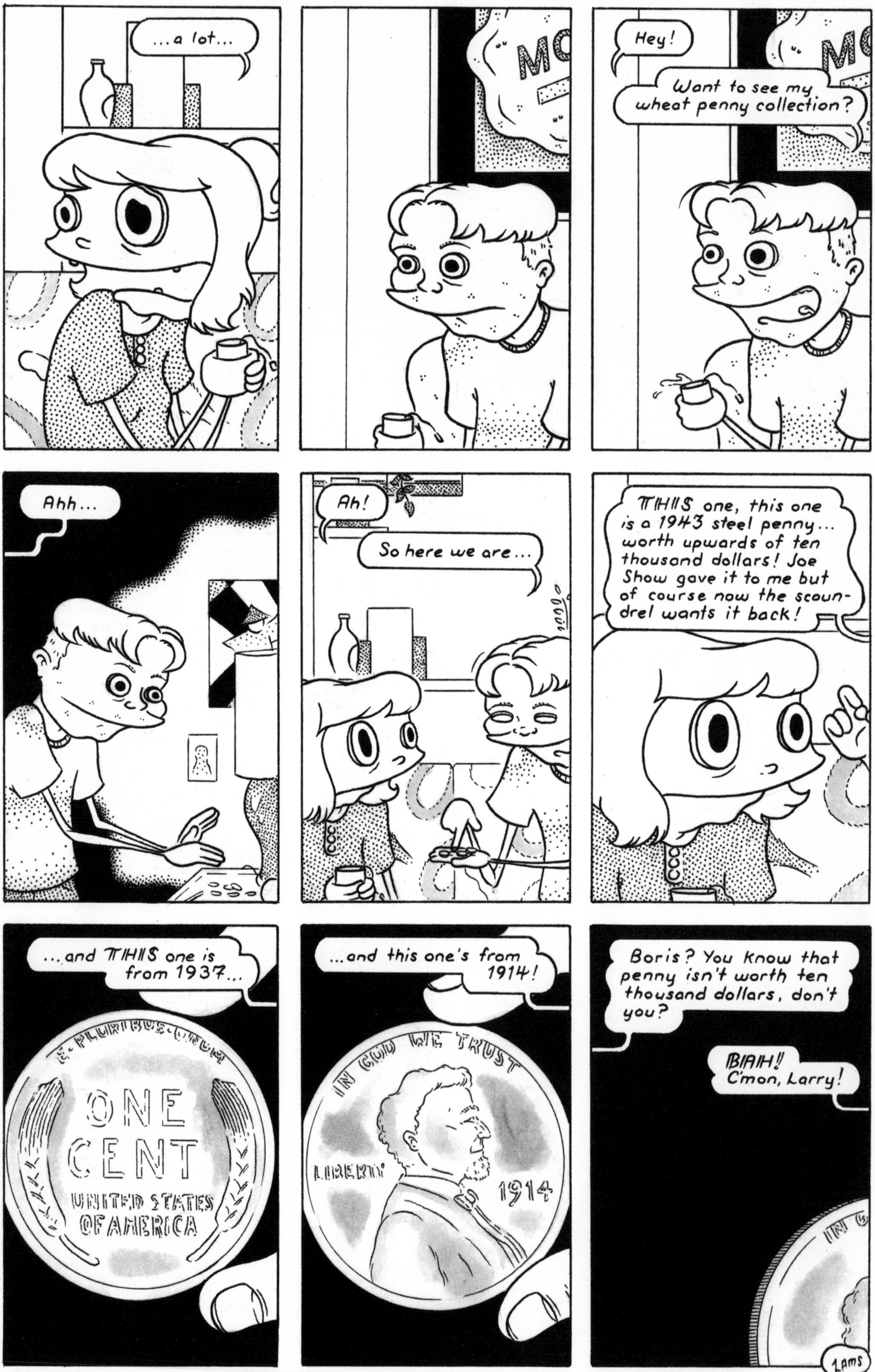
...a lot...
Hey!
Want to see my wheat penny collection?
Ahh...
Ah!
So here we are...
THIS one, this one is a 1943 steel penny... worth upwards of ten thousand dollars! Joe Show gave it to me but of course now the scoundrel wants it back!
...and THIS one is from 1937...
ONE CENT
UNITED STATES OF AMERICA
...and this one's from 1914!
IN GOD WE TRUST
LIBERTY
1914
Boris? You know that penny isn't worth ten thousand dollars, don't you?
BAH!! C'mon, Larry!

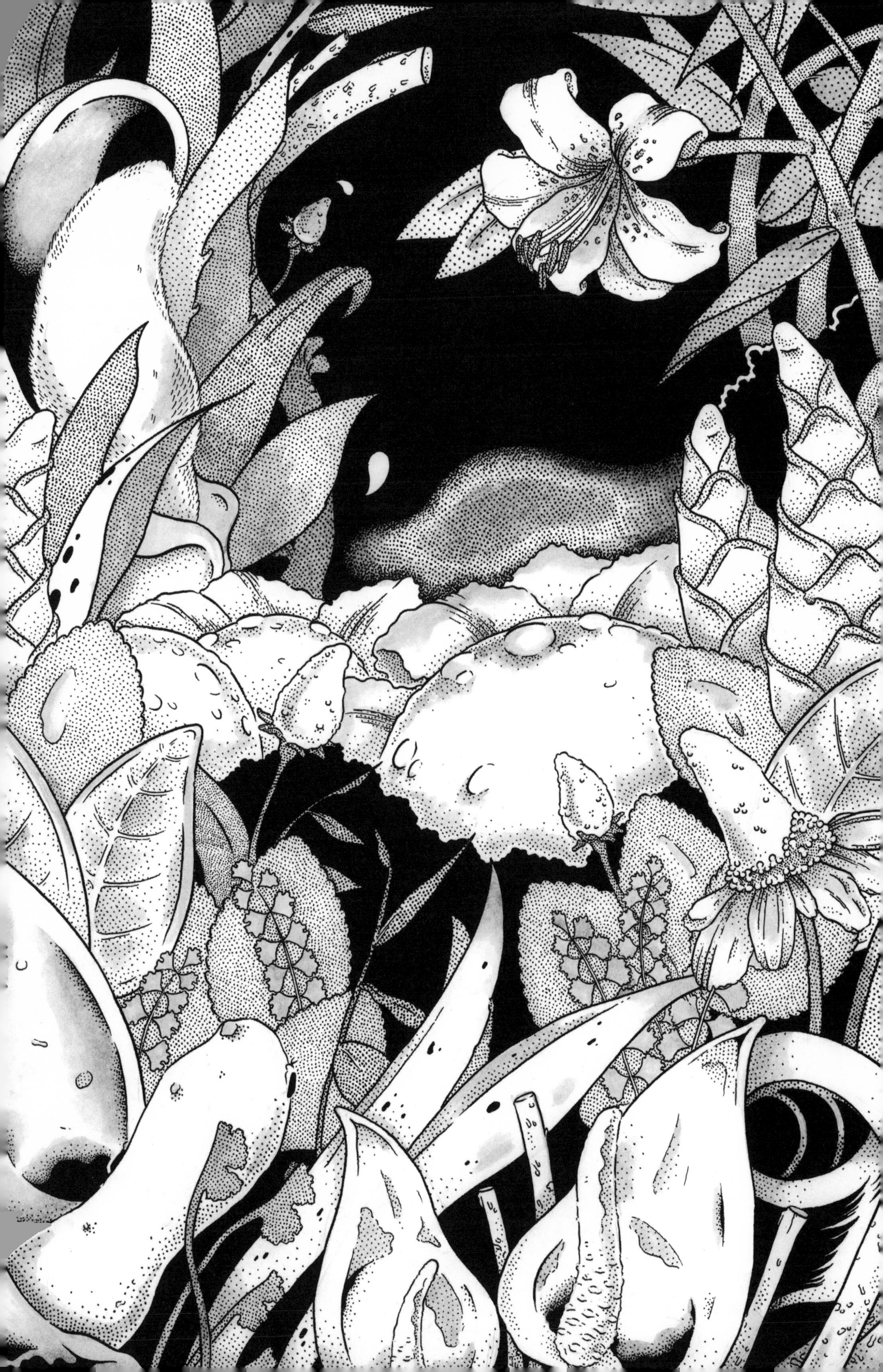

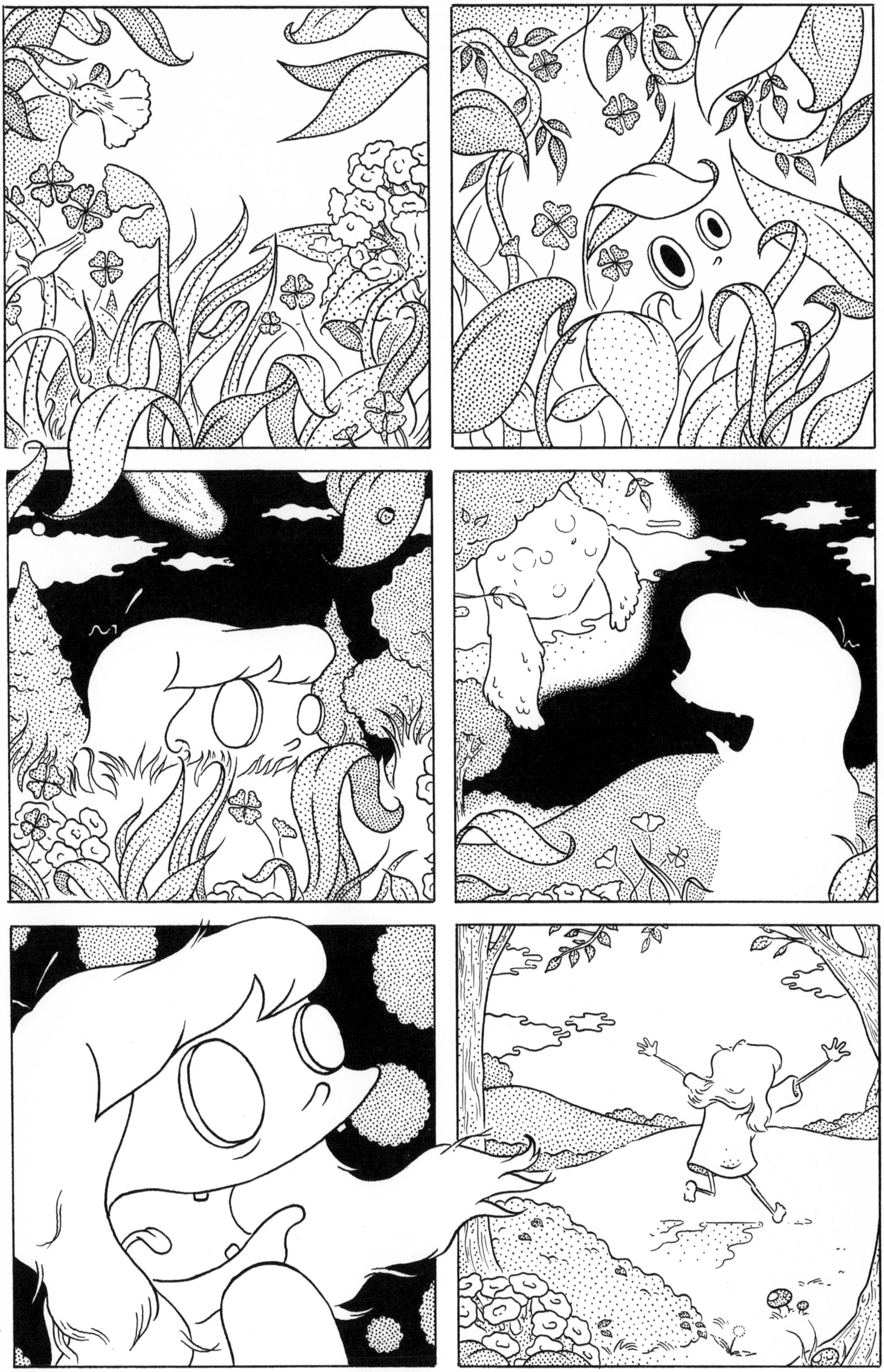

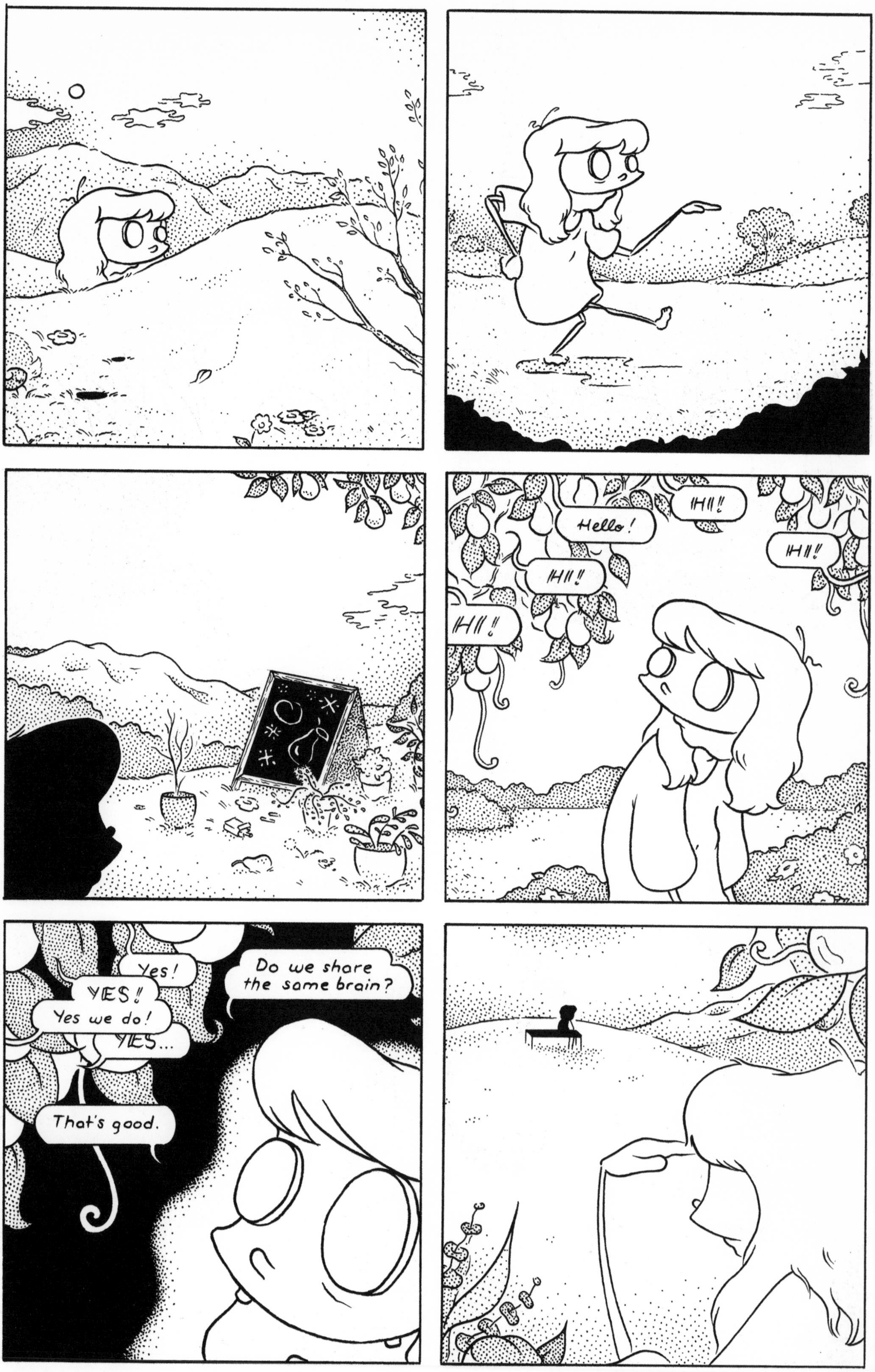
Hello!
HI!!
HI!!
HI!!
HI!!
HI!!
Do we share the same brain?
Yes!
YES!!
Yes we do!
YES...
That's good.

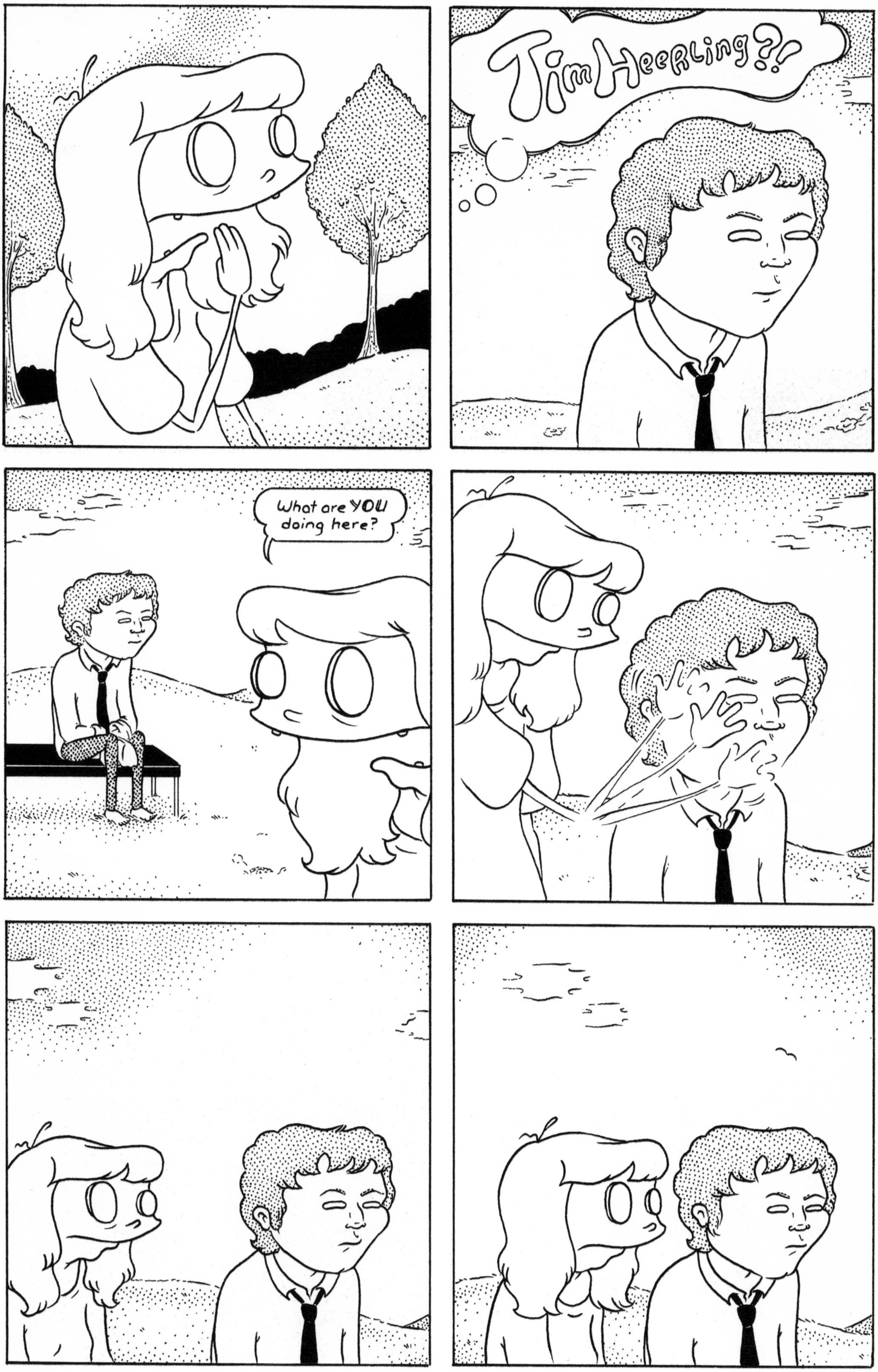
Tim Heerling?!
What are YOU doing here?

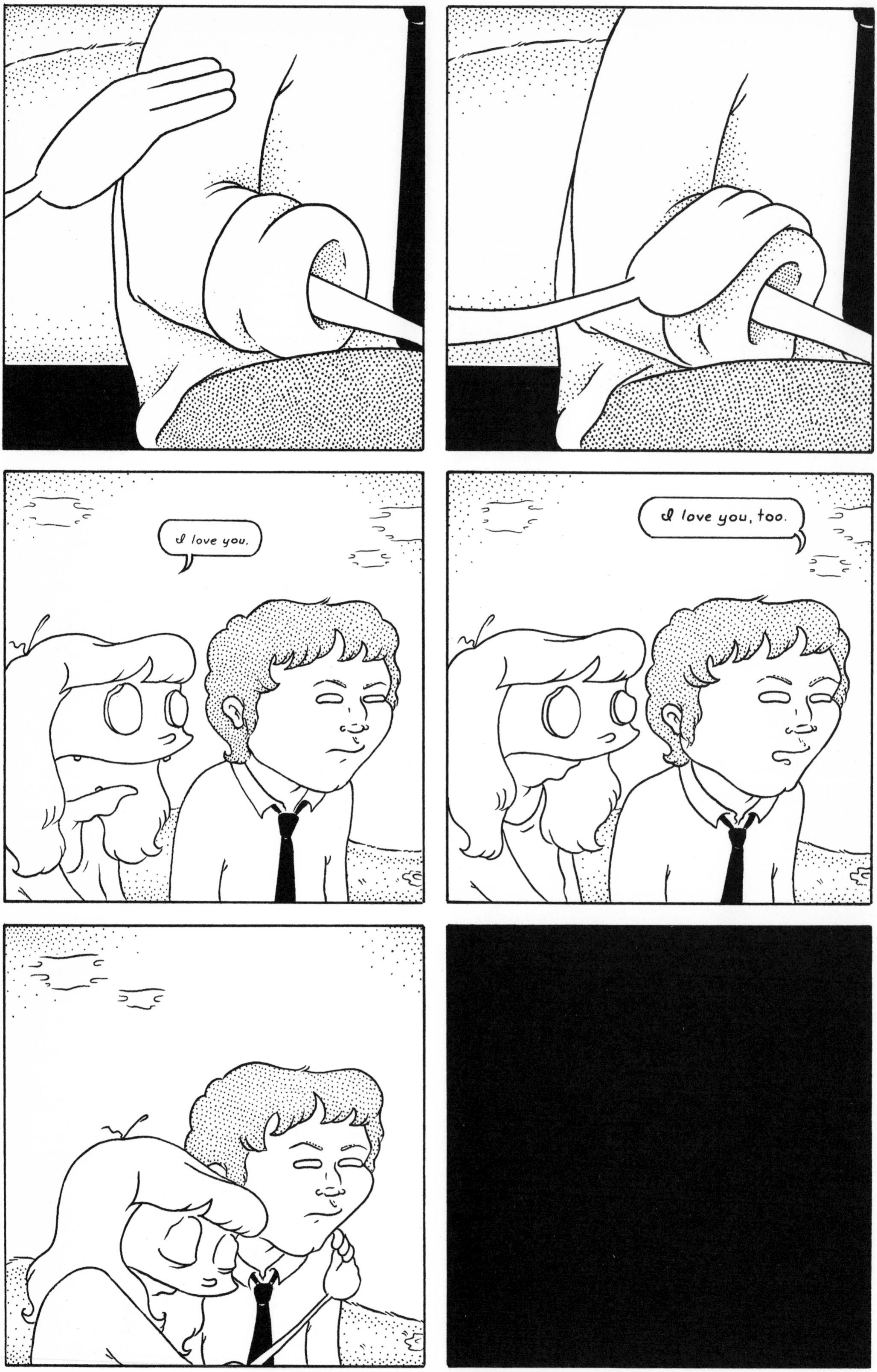
I love you.
I love you, too.

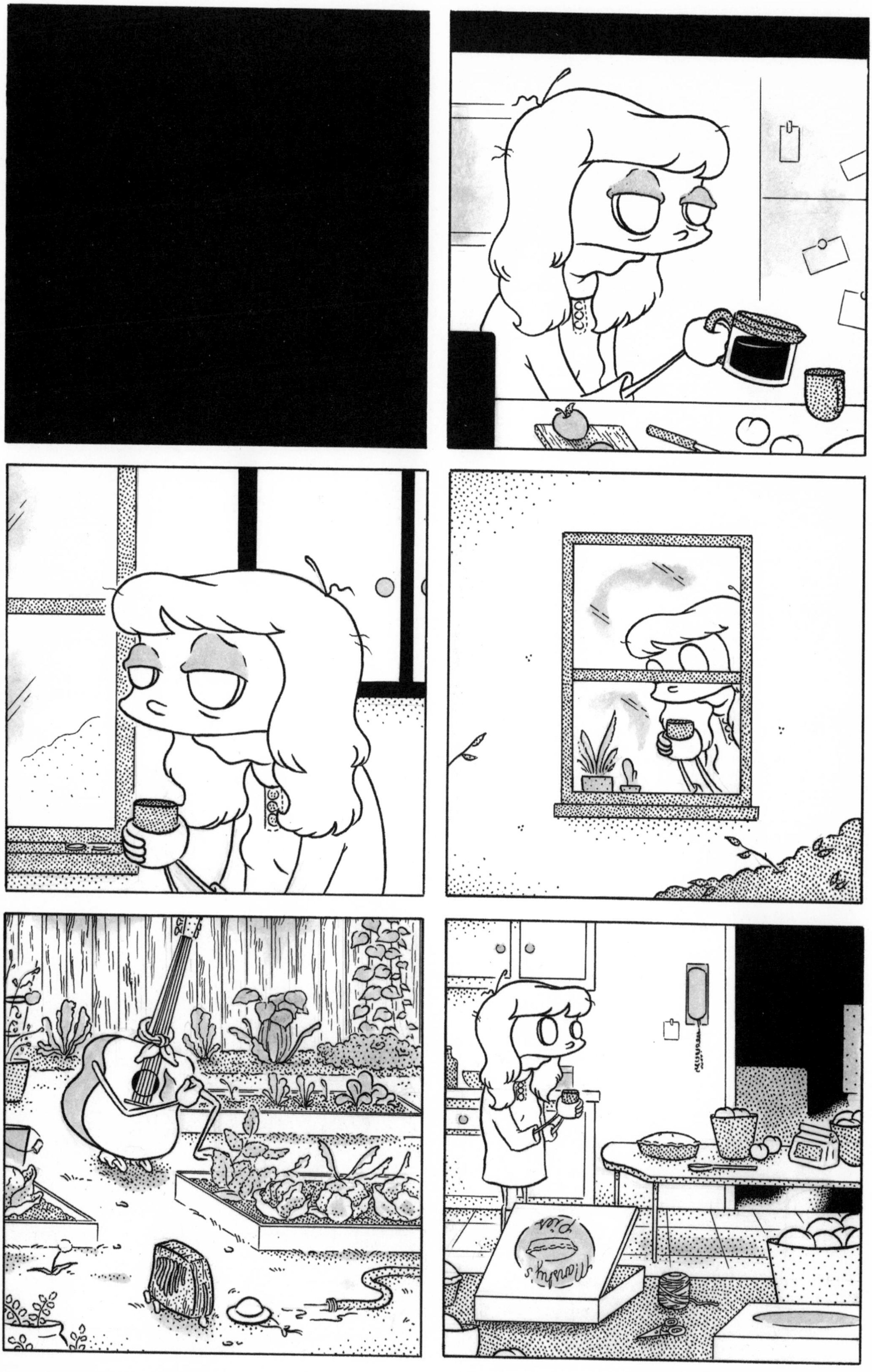
Pies

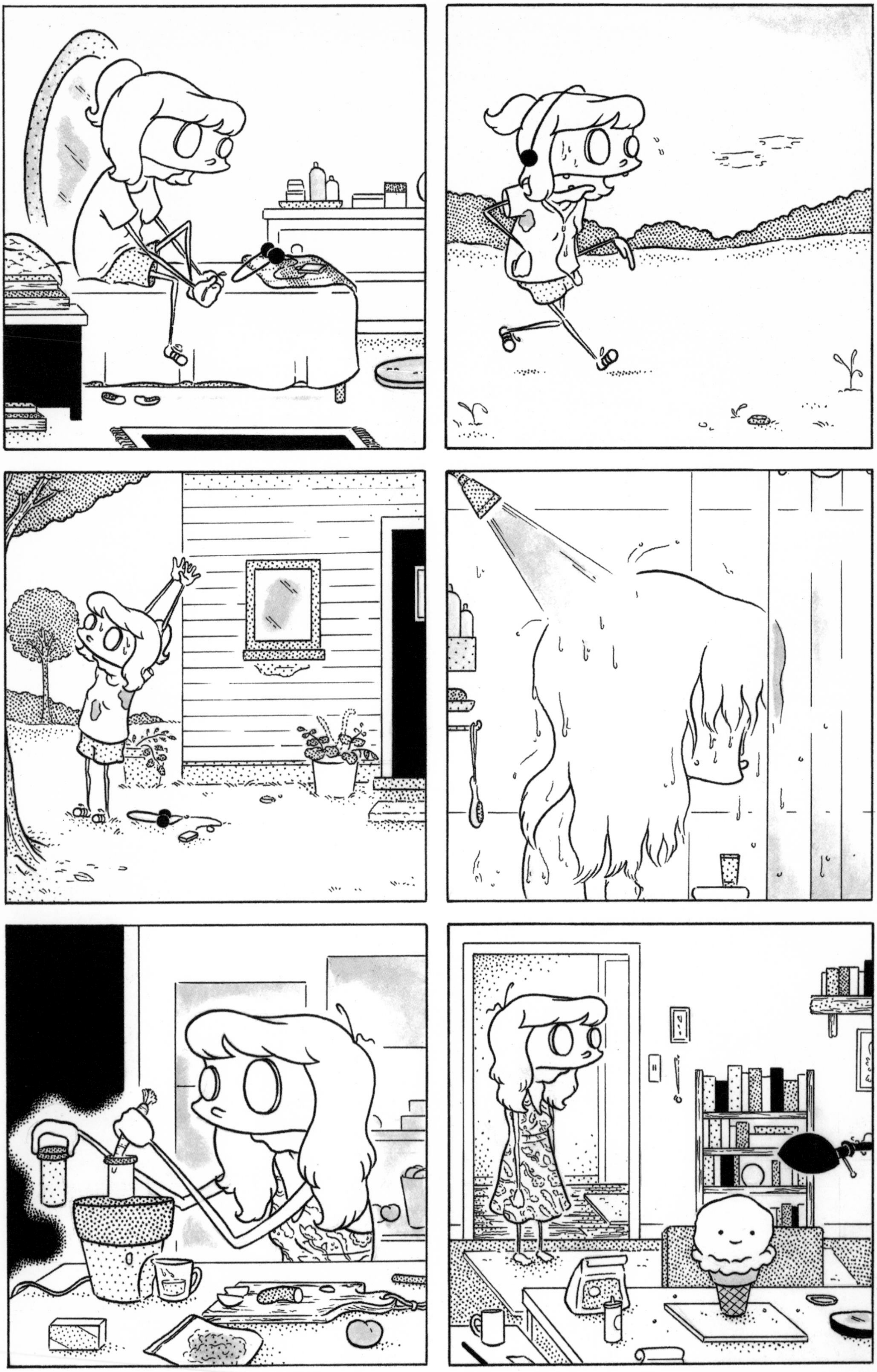

That was supposed to help...

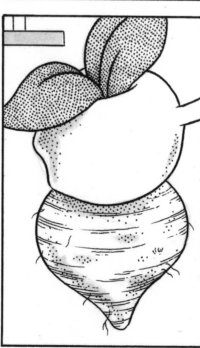

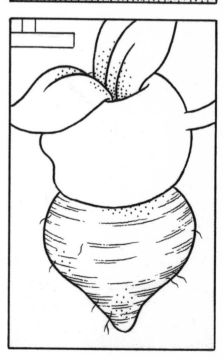

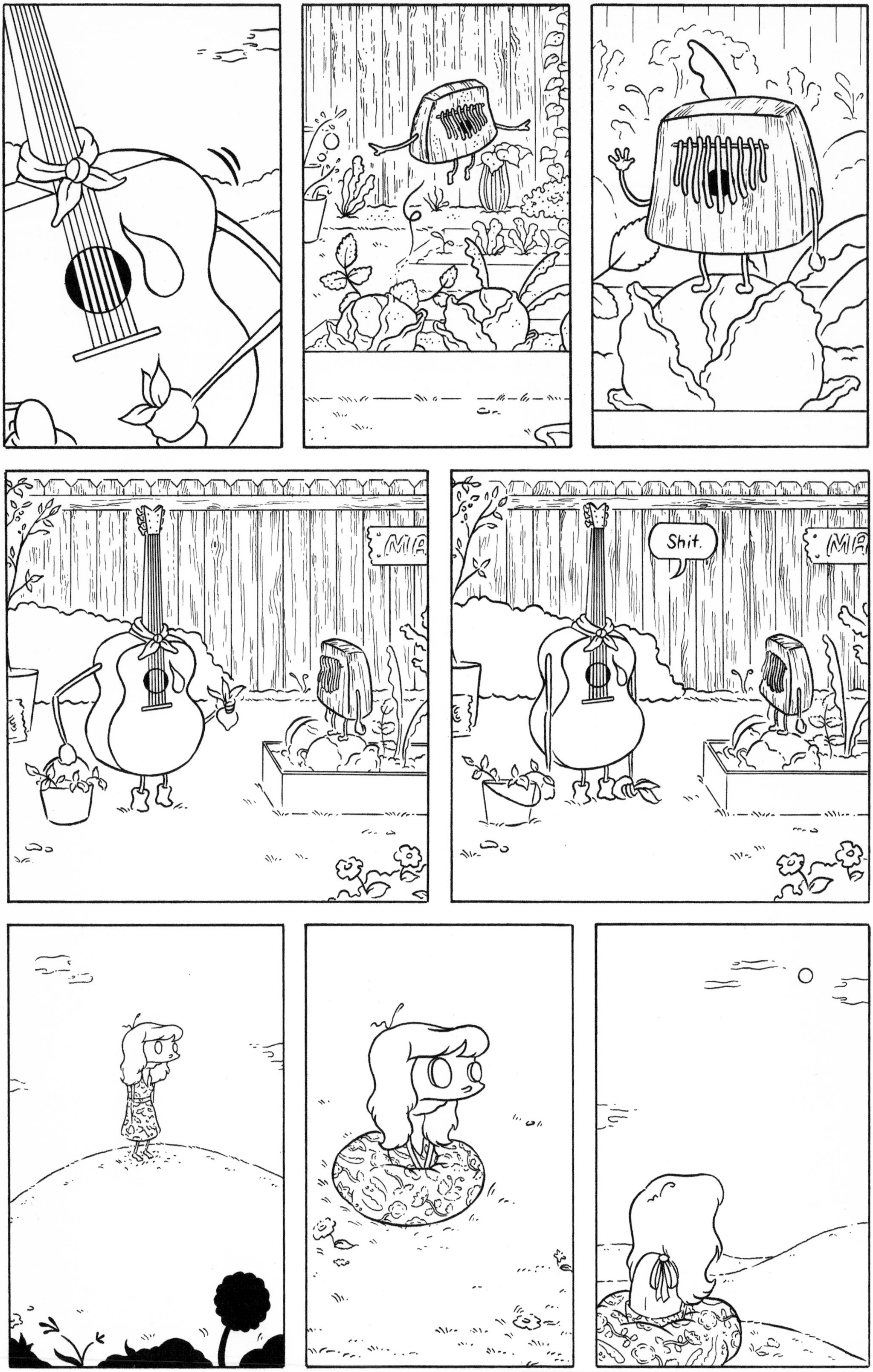
Shit.

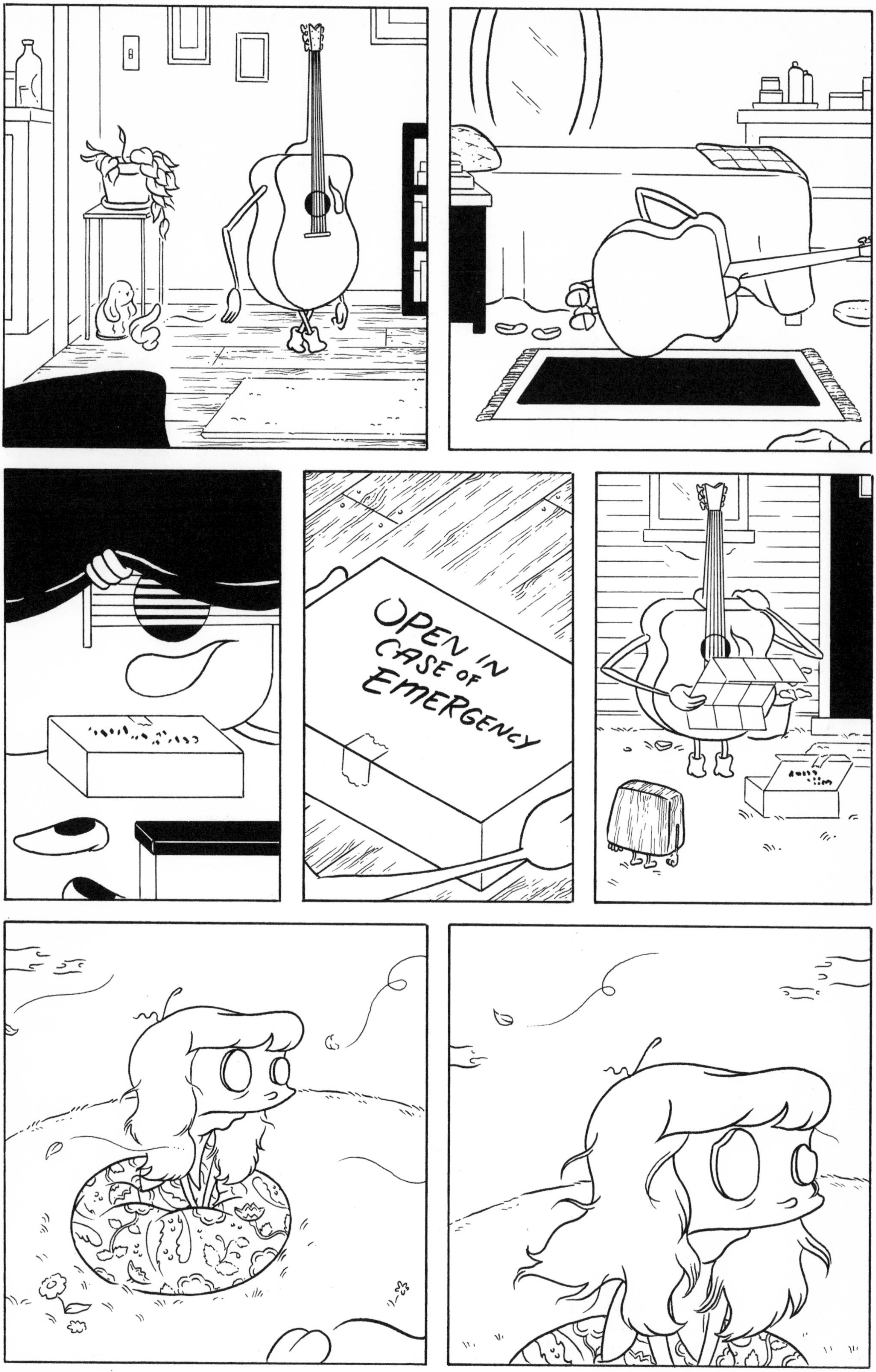
OPEN IN CASE OF EMERGENCY

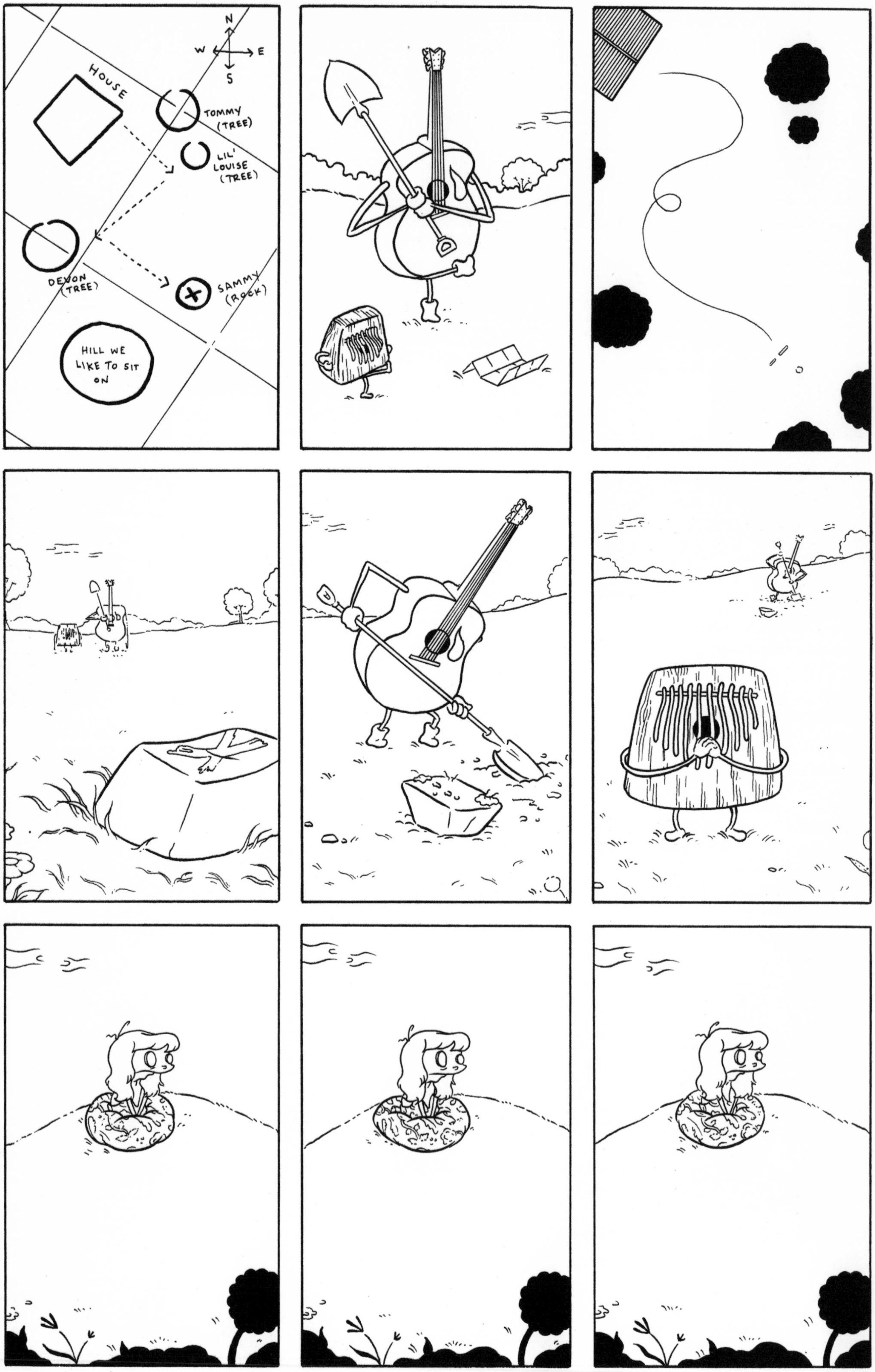
N
W
E
S
HOUSE
TOMMY (TREE)
LIL' LOUISE (TREE)
DEVON (TREE)
SAMMY (ROCK)
HILL WE LIKE TO SIT ON

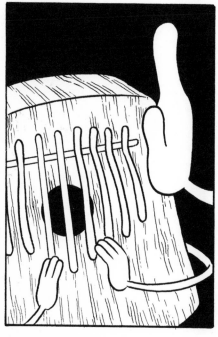

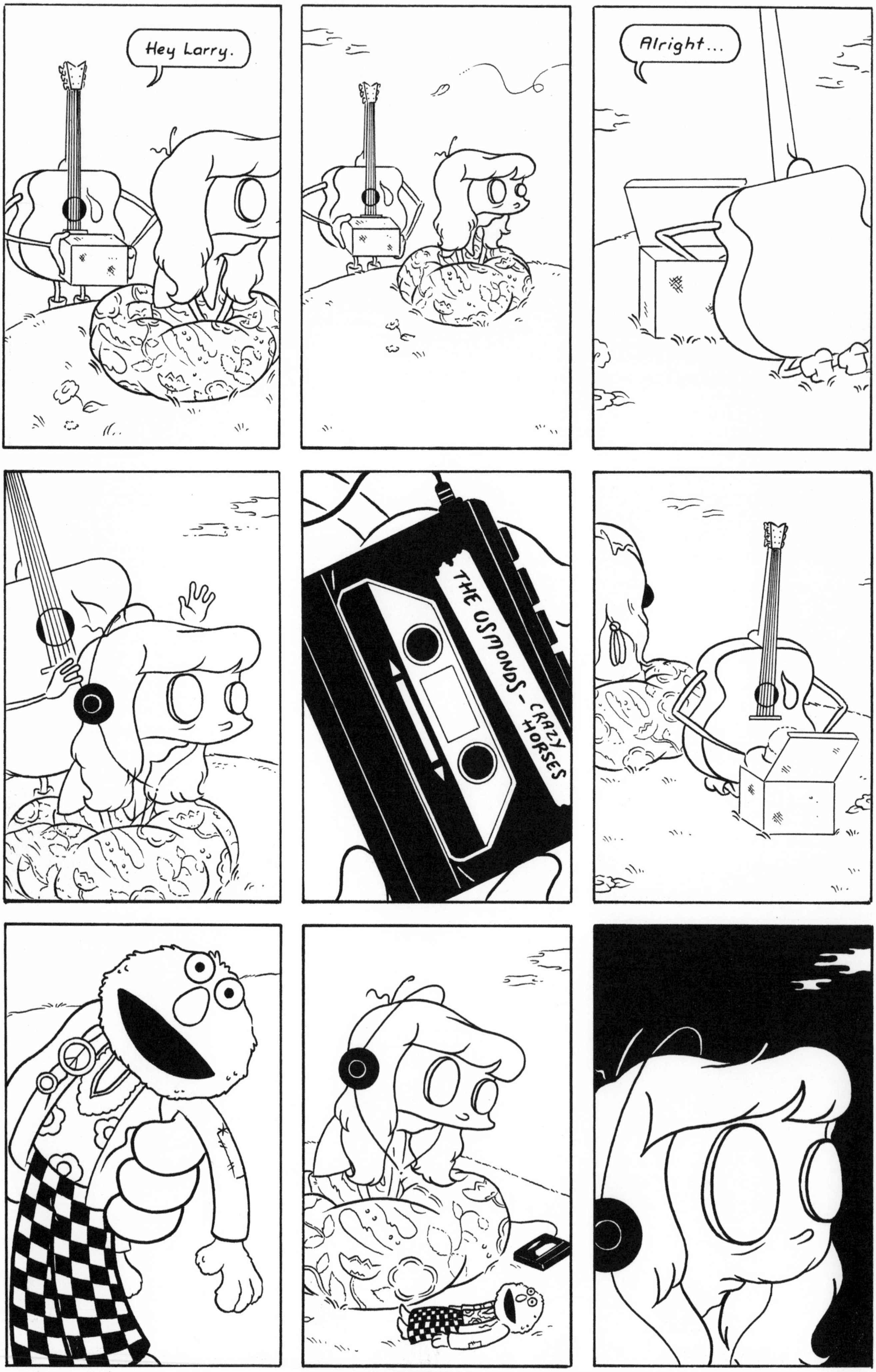
Hey Larry.
Alright...
THE OSMONDS - CRAZY HORSES

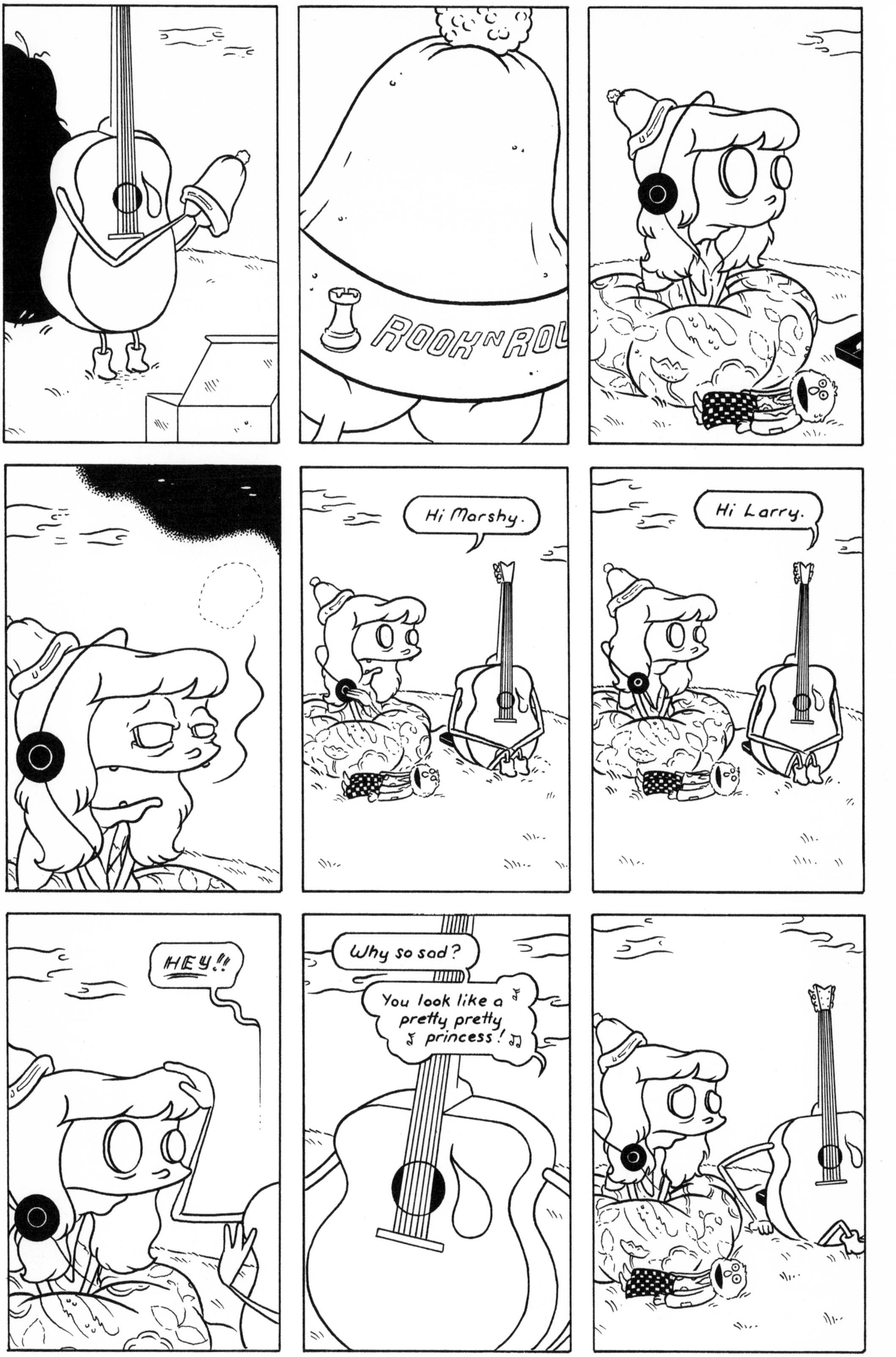

ROOK N ROLL
Hi Marshy.
Hi Larry.
HEY!!
Why so sad?
You look like a pretty pretty princess!

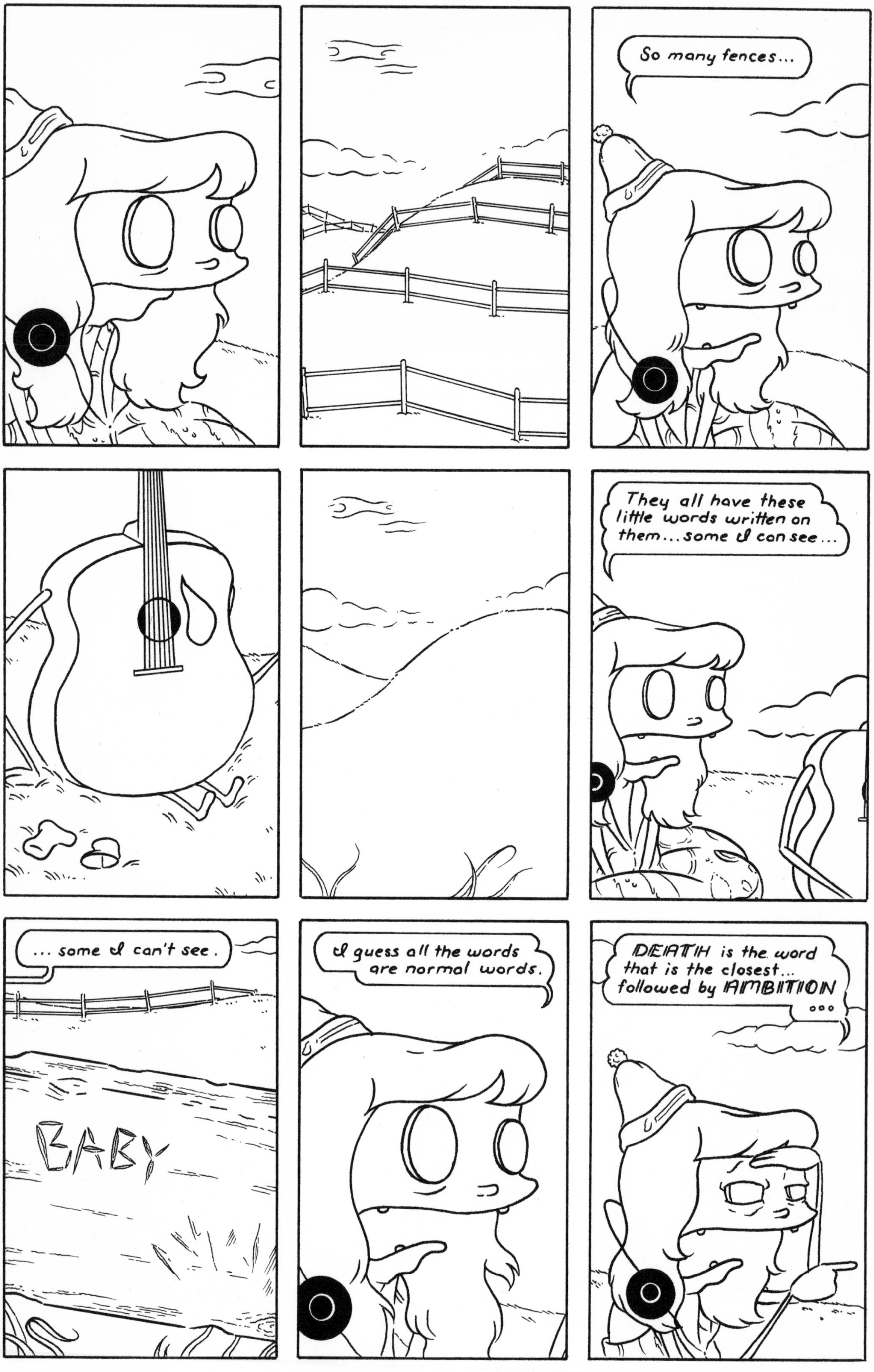
So many fences...
They all have these little words written on them... some I can see...
... some I can't see.
BABY
I guess all the words are normal words.
DEATH is the word that is the closest... followed by AMBITION
...

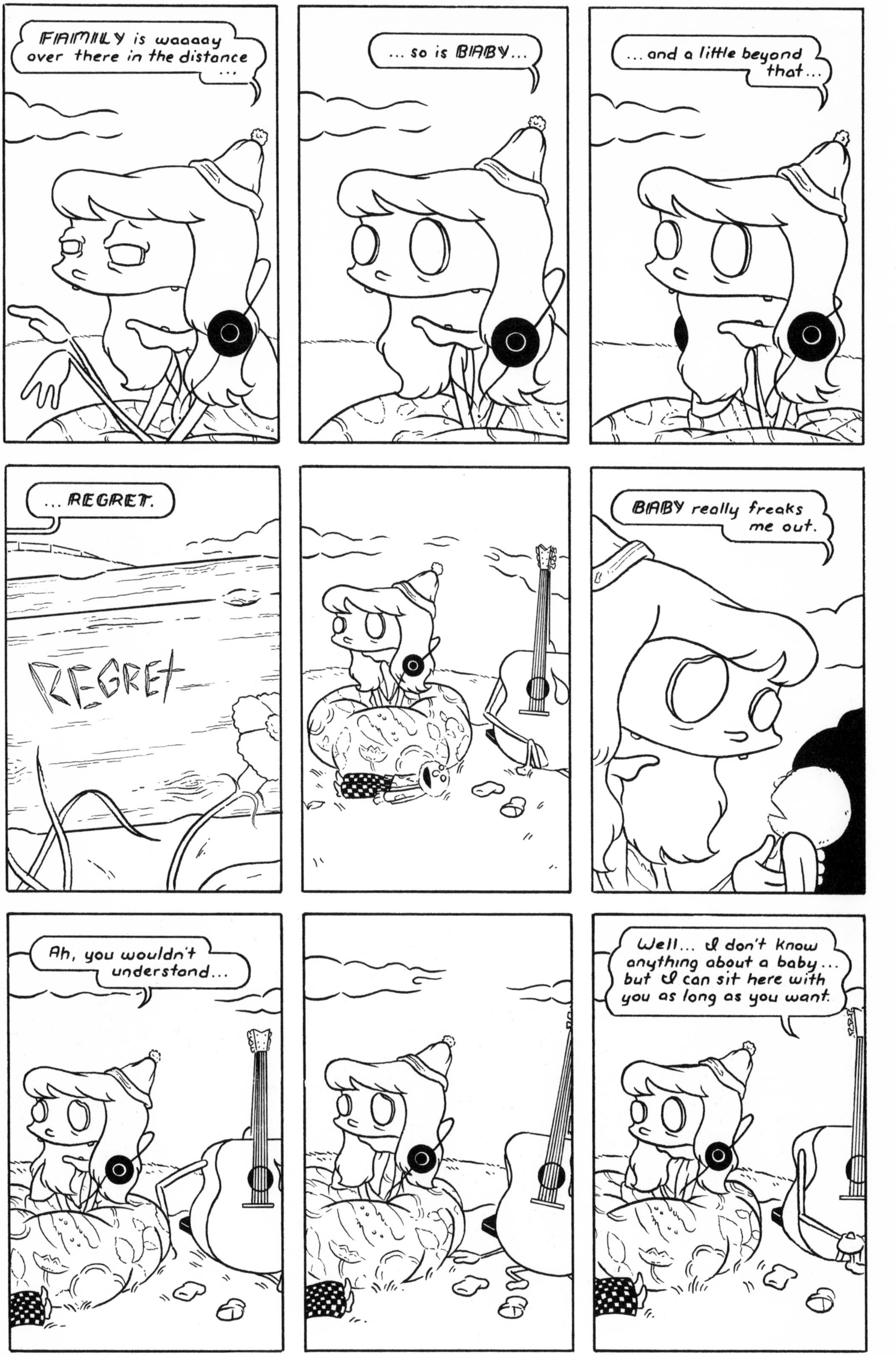
FAMILY is waaaay over there in the distance . . .
. . . so is BABY . . .
. . . and a little beyond that . . .
. . . REGRET.
REGRET
BABY really freaks me out.
Ah, you wouldn't understand . . .
Well . . . I don't know anything about a baby . . . but I can sit here with you as long as you want.

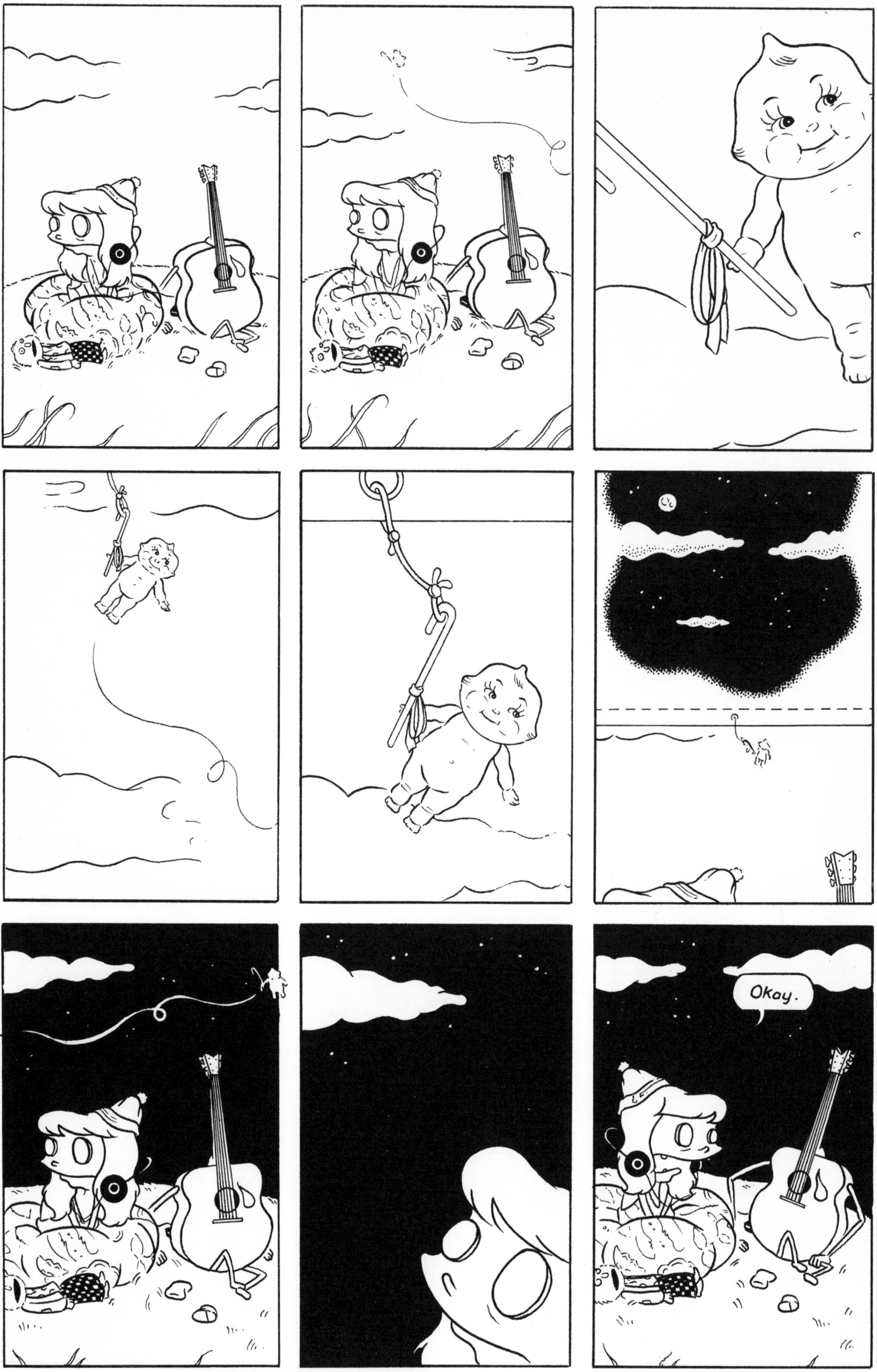
Okay.

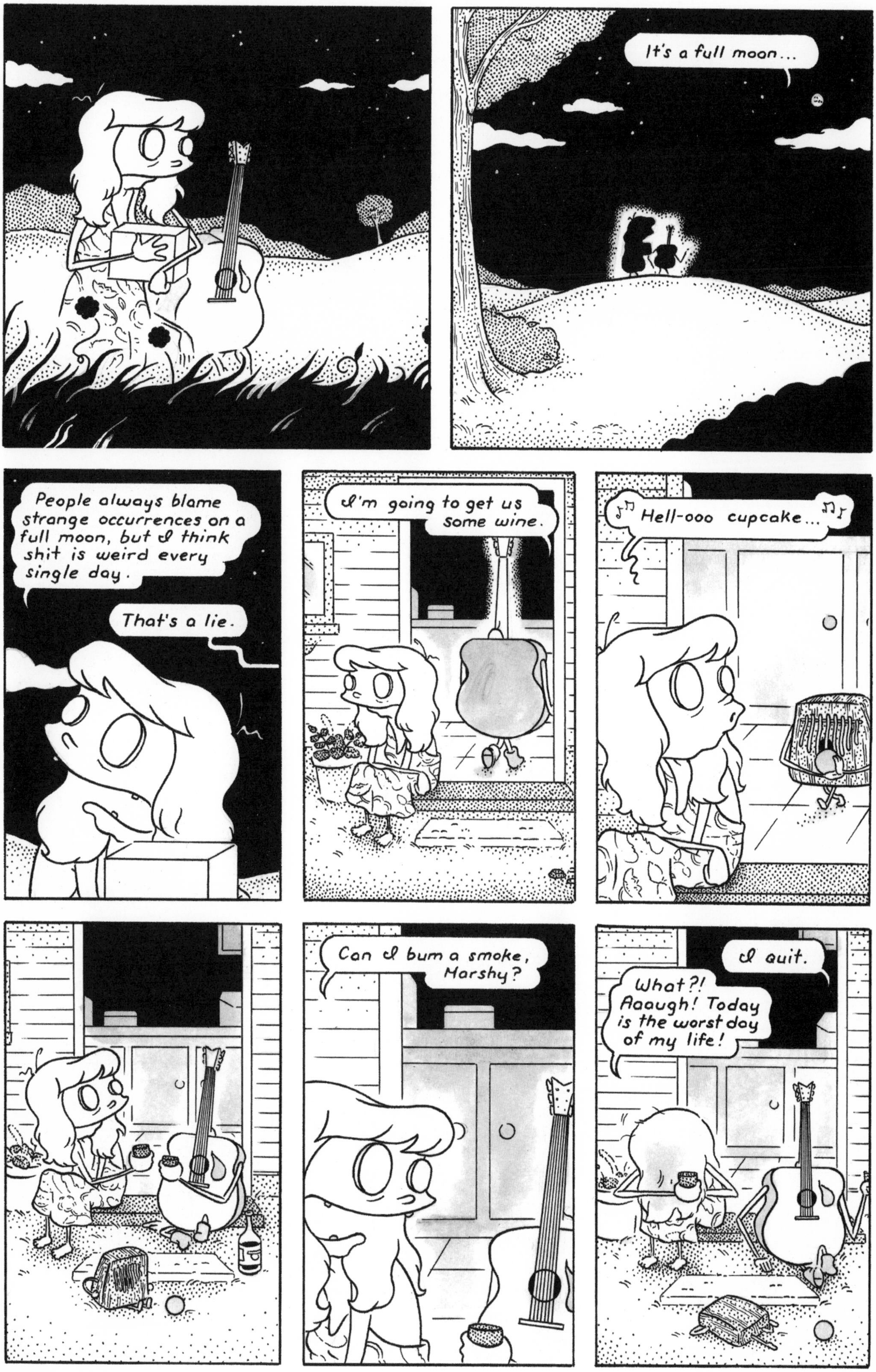
It's a full moon...
People always blame strange occurrences on a full moon, but I think shit is weird every single day.
That's a lie.
I'm going to get us some wine.
Hell-ooo cupcake...
Can I bum a smoke, Marshy?
I quit.
What?! Aaaugh! Today is the worst day of my life!

BBRRIIIIING!!
BBRRIIIIING!!
Hello?
Uh huh...
Oh hi, how are you?
Oh, really?
Oh, that's nice of you to say...
12
3
6
9
Okay, well...
Yes, I'll let you know in a few days...

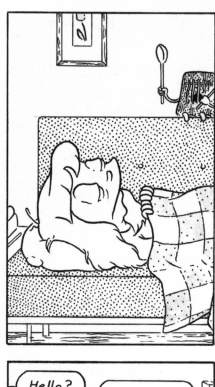

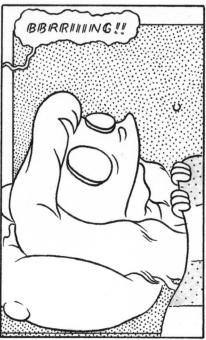

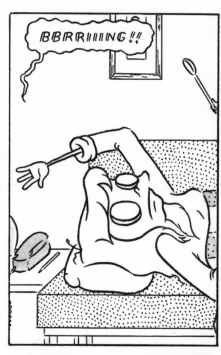

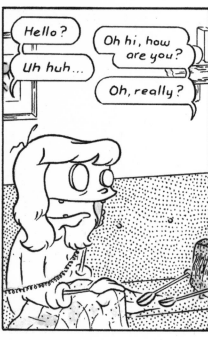

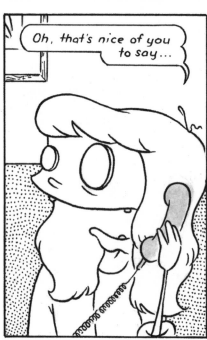

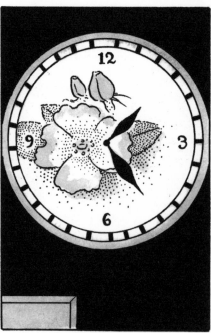

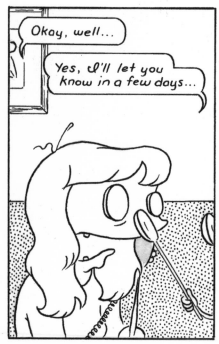

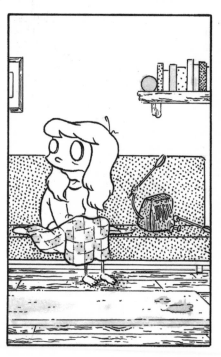

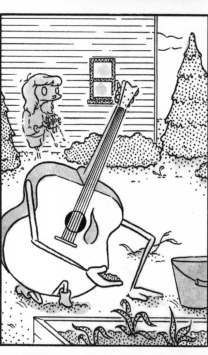

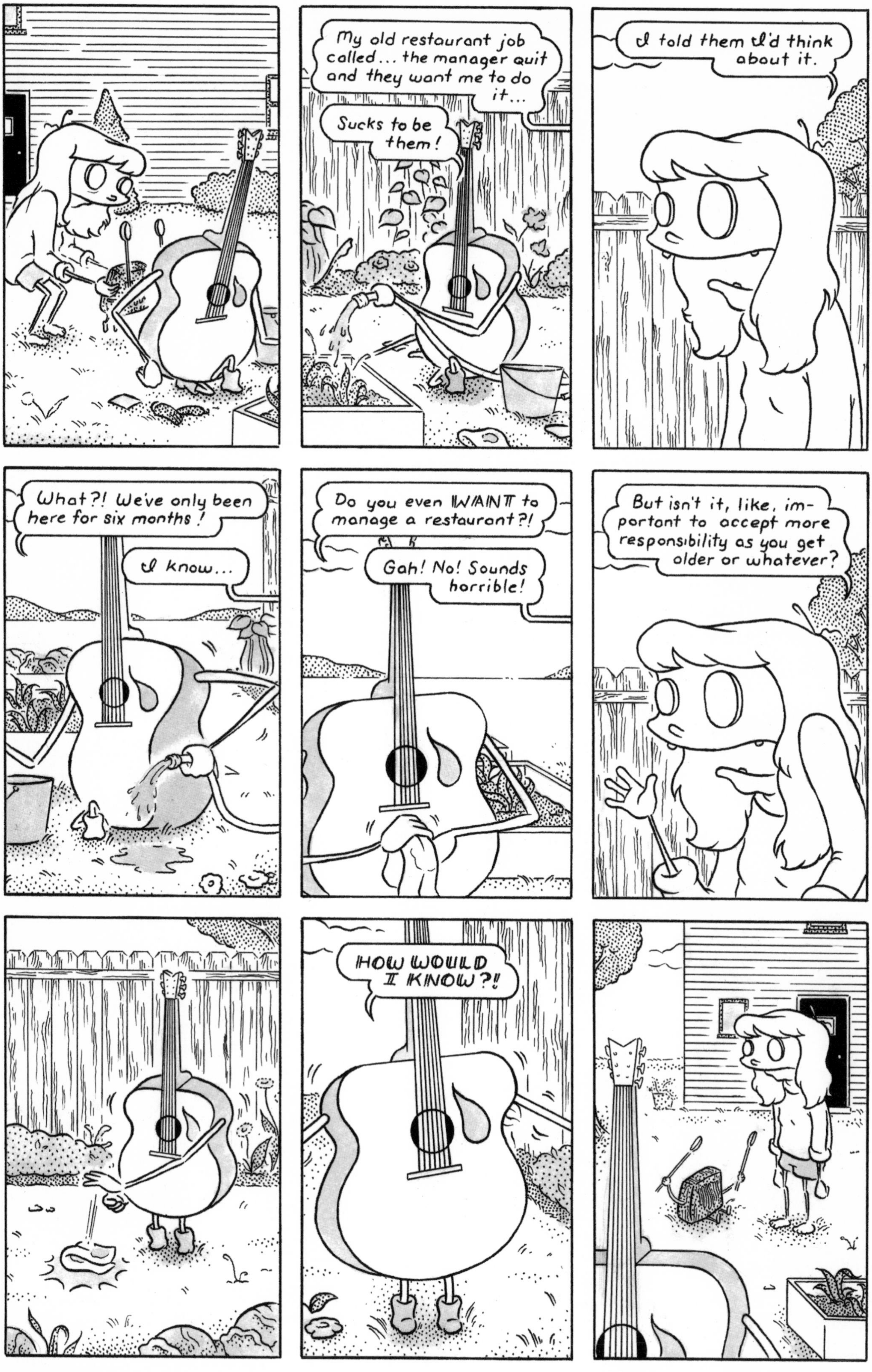

My old restaurant job called... the manager quit and they want me to do it...
Sucks to be them!
I told them I'd think about it.
What?! We've only been here for six months!
I know...
Do you even WANT to manage a restaurant?!
Gah! No! Sounds horrible!
But isn't it, like, important to accept more responsibility as you get older or whatever?
HOW WOULD I KNOW?!

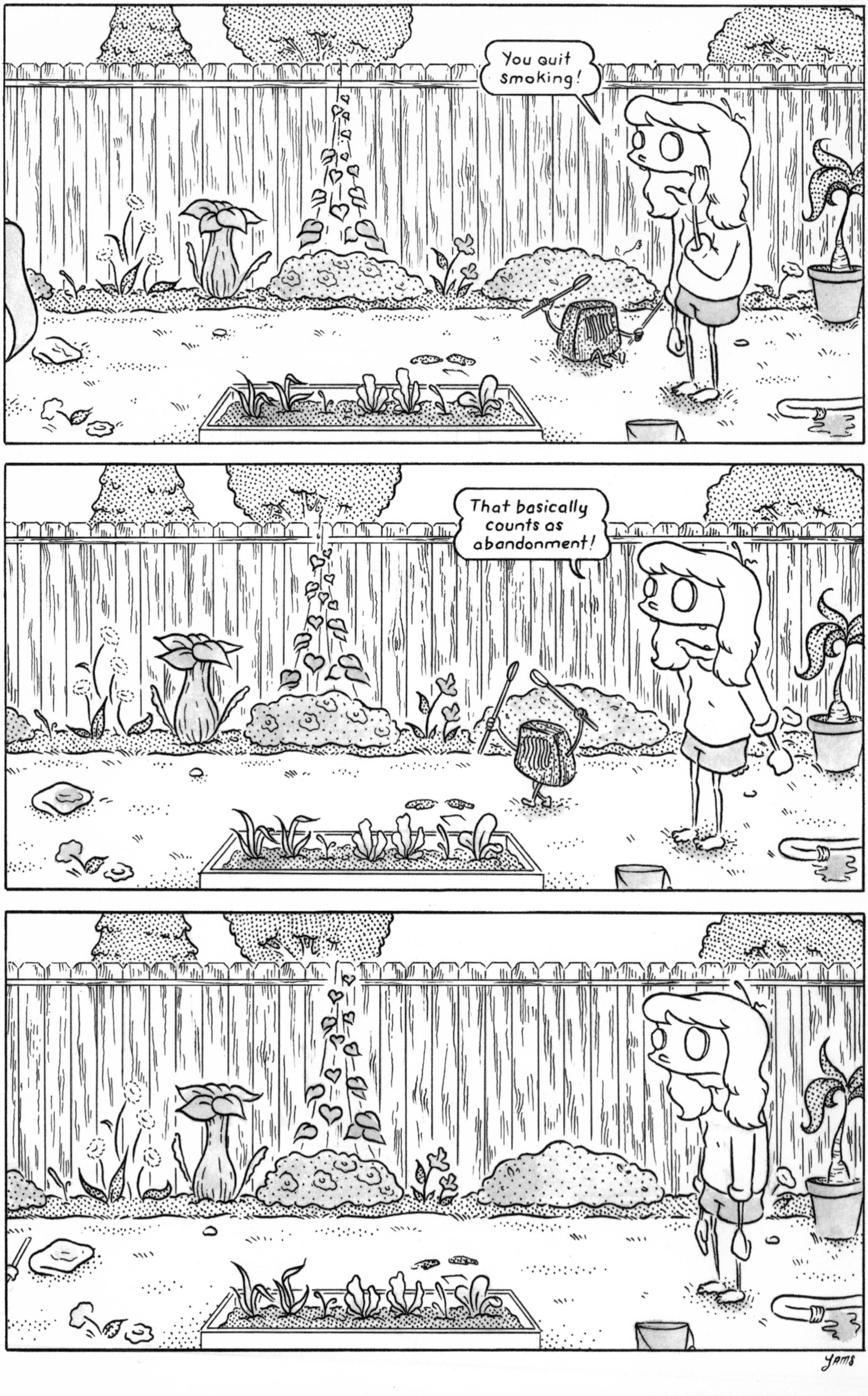
You quit smoking!
That basically counts as abandonment!
Yams

BOY

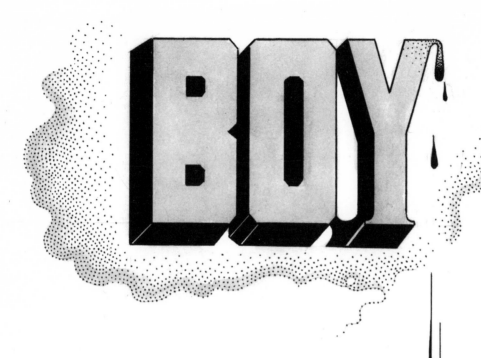

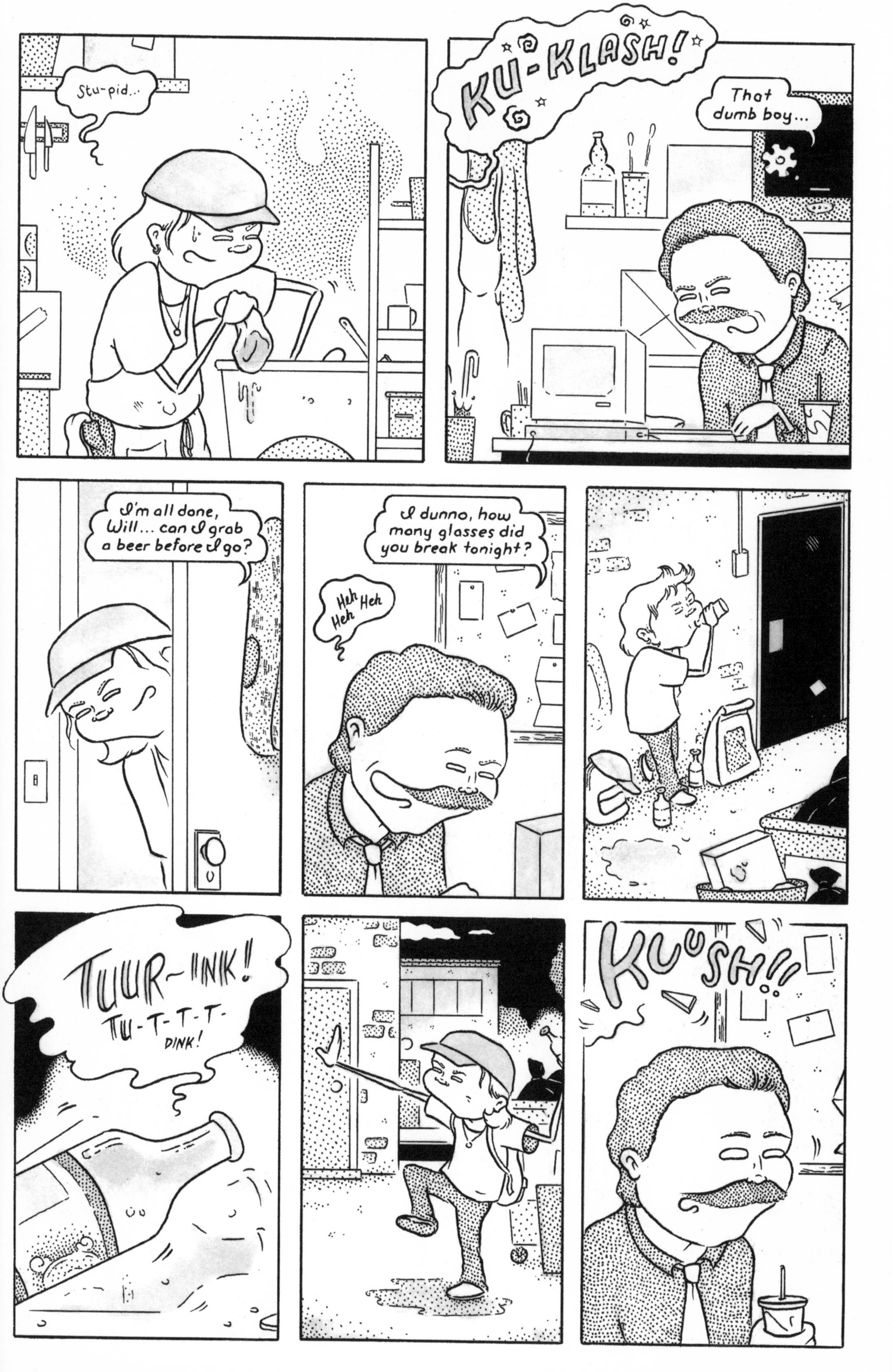
Stu-pid...
KU-KLASH!
That dumb boy...
I'm all done, Will... can I grab a beer before I go?
I dunno, how many glasses did you break tonight?
Heh Heh Heh
TUUR-INK!
TU-T-T-T-
DINK!
KUUSH!!

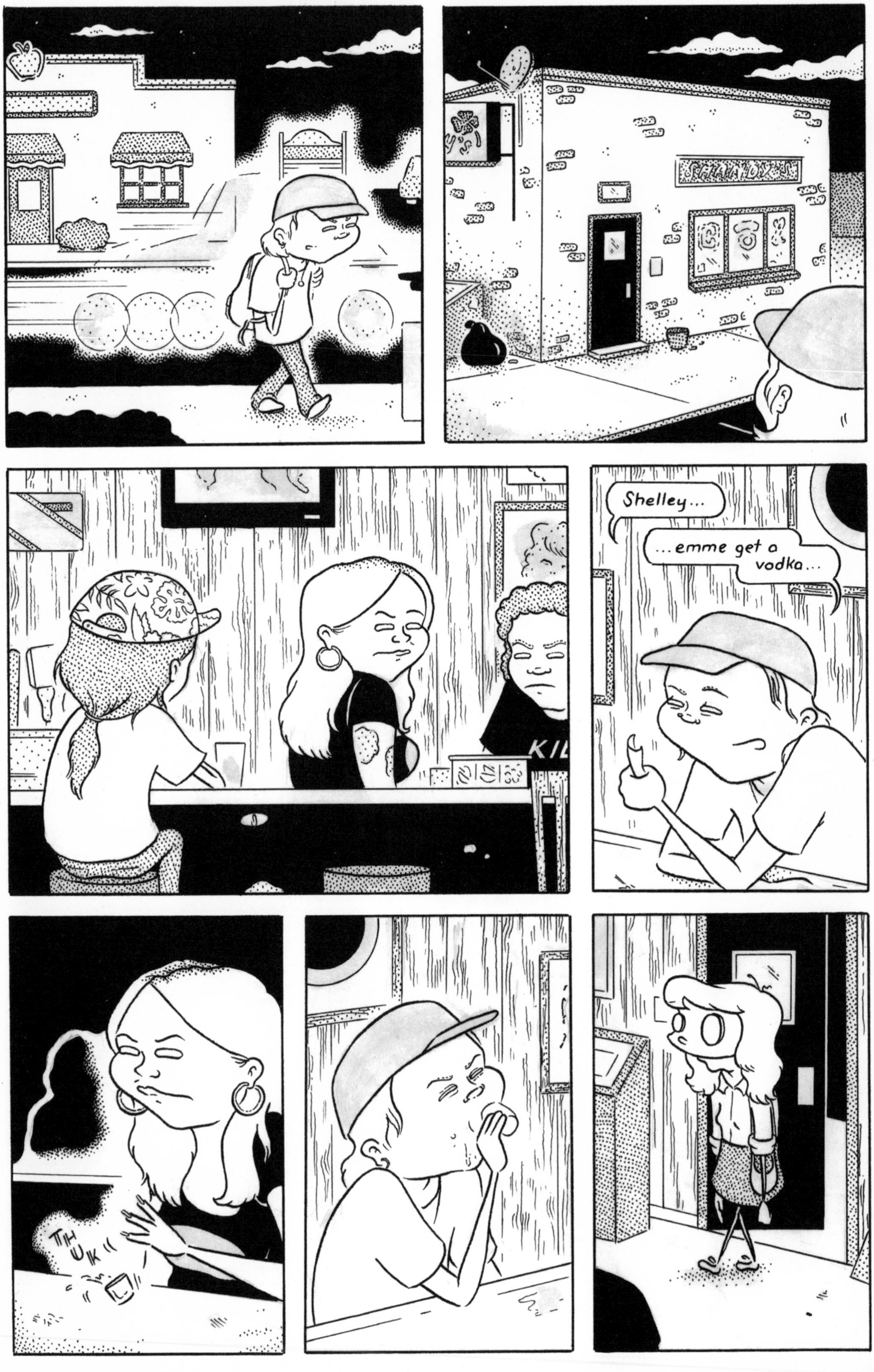
SHANDY'S
Shelley...
...emme get a vodka...
THUK

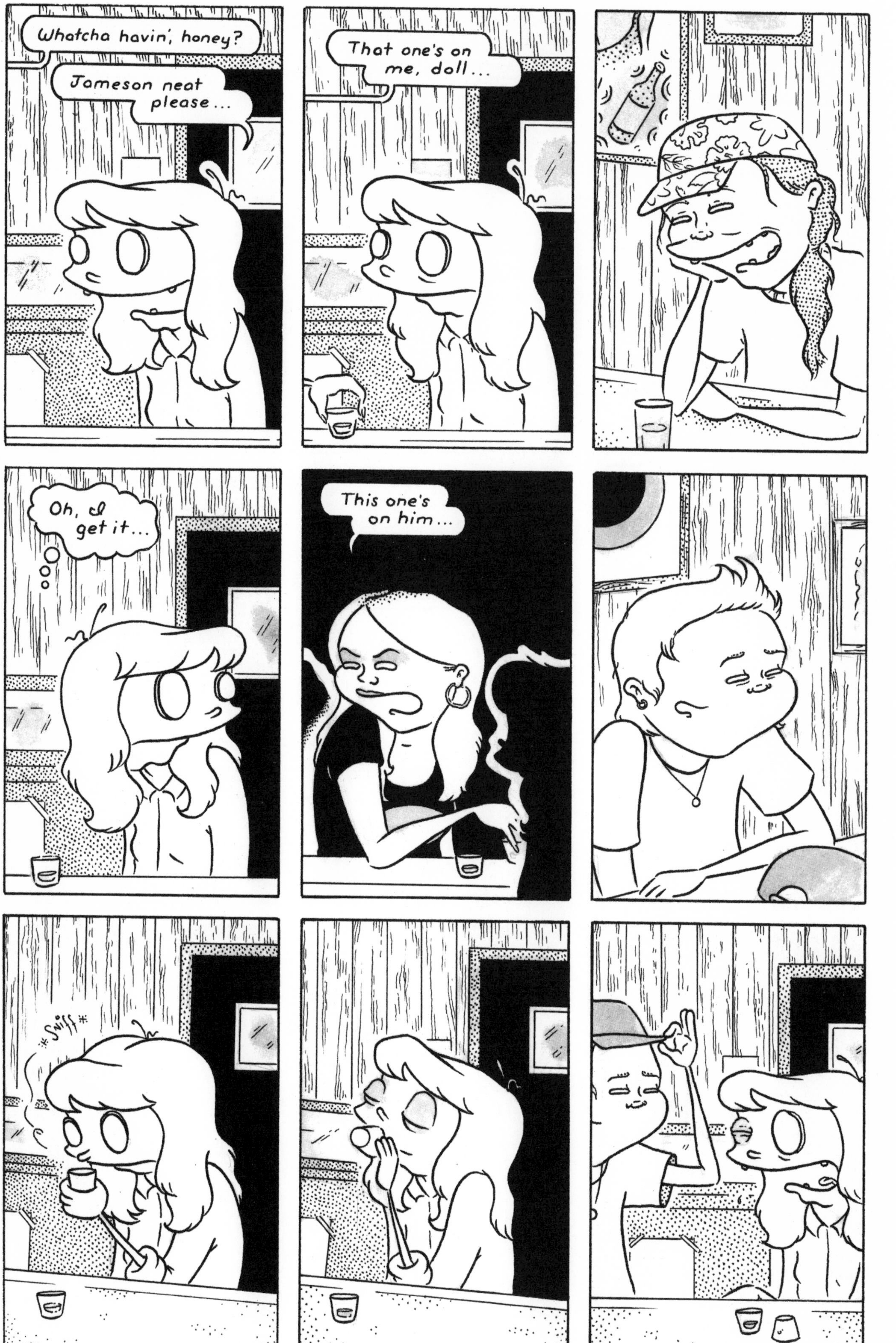
Whatcha havin', honey?
Jameson neat please...
That one's on me, doll...
Oh, I get it...
This one's on him...
Sniff

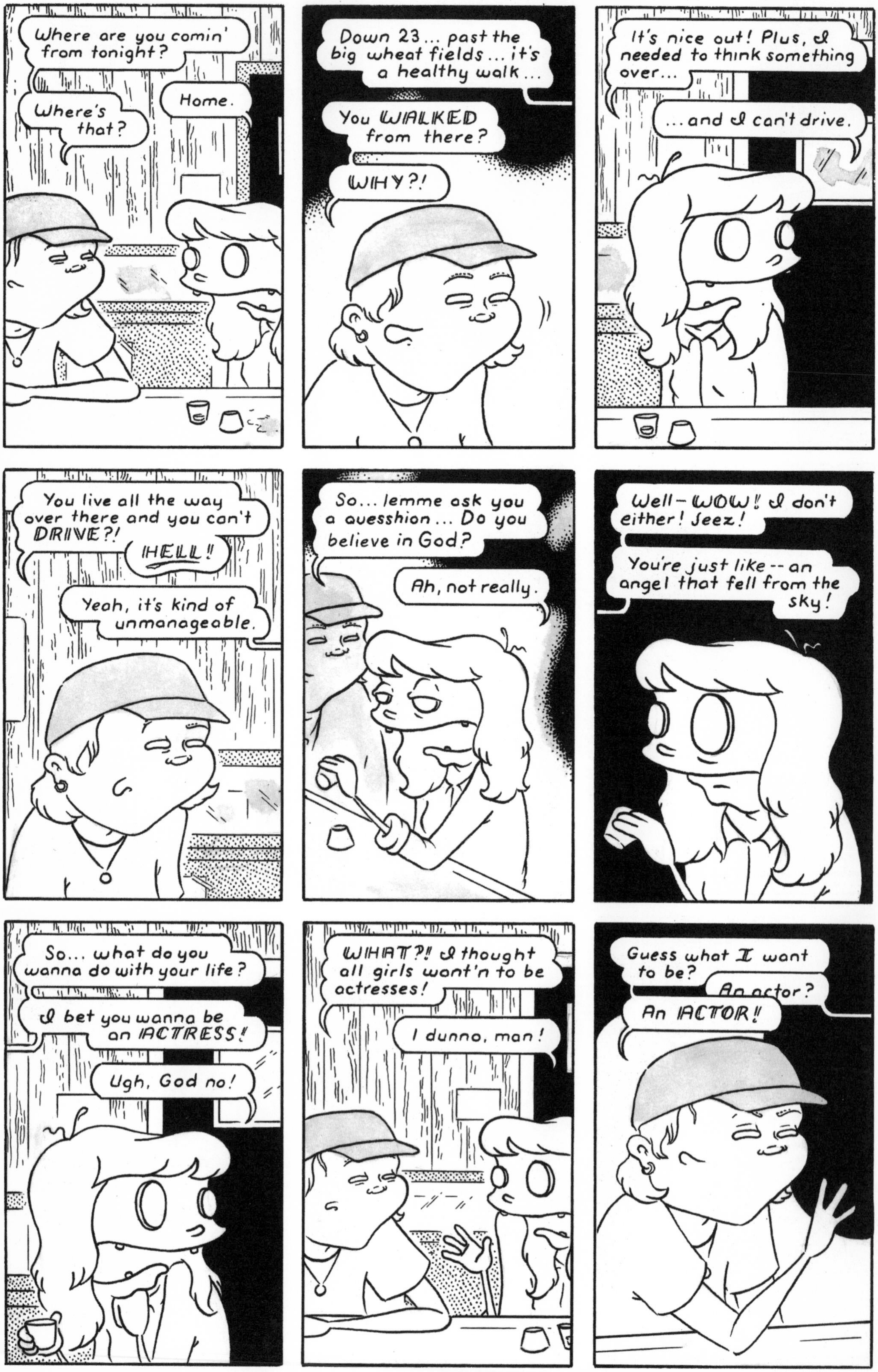
Where are you comin' from tonight?
Home.
Where's that?
Down 23... past the big wheat fields... it's a healthy walk...
You WALKED from there?
WHY?!
It's nice out! Plus, I needed to think something over...
...and I can't drive.
You live all the way over there and you can't DRIVE?!
HELL!
Yeah, it's kind of unmanageable.
So... lemme ask you a quesshion... Do you believe in God?
Ah, not really.
Well- WOW! I don't either! Jeez!
You're just like--an angel that fell from the sky!
So... what do you wanna do with your life?
I bet you wanna be an ACTRESS!
Ugh, God no!
WHAT?! I thought all girls want'n to be actresses!
I dunno, man!
Guess what I want to be?
An actor?
An ACTOR!!

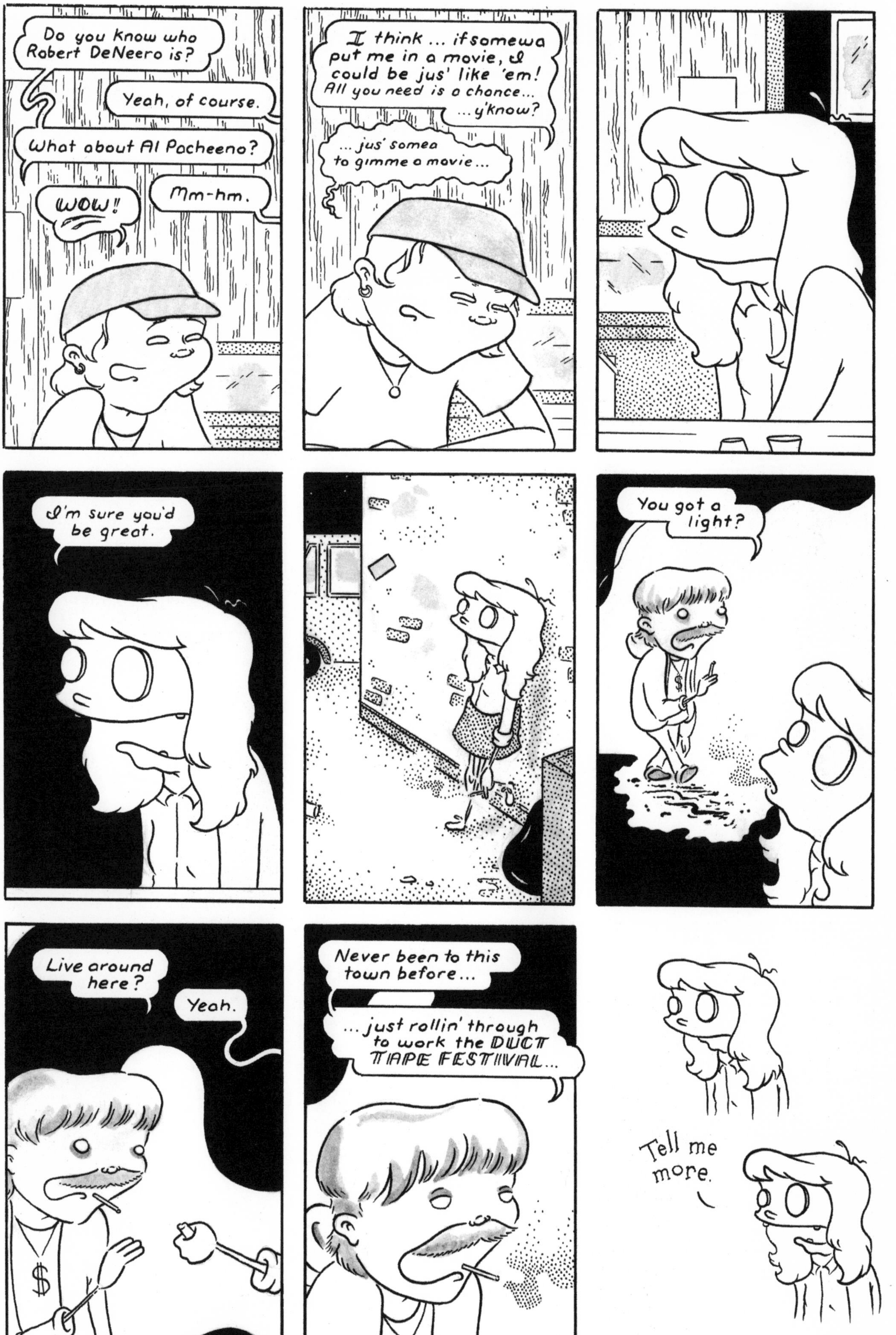
Do you know who Robert DeNeero is?
Yeah, of course.
What about Al Pacheeno?
Mm-hm.
WOW!!
I think ... if somewa put me in a movie, I could be jus' like 'em! All you need is a chance...
...y'know?
... jus' somea to gimme a movie ...
I'm sure you'd be great.
You got a light?
Live around here?
Yeah.
Never been to this town before...
... just rollin' through to work the DUCT TAPE FESTIVAL...
Tell me more.

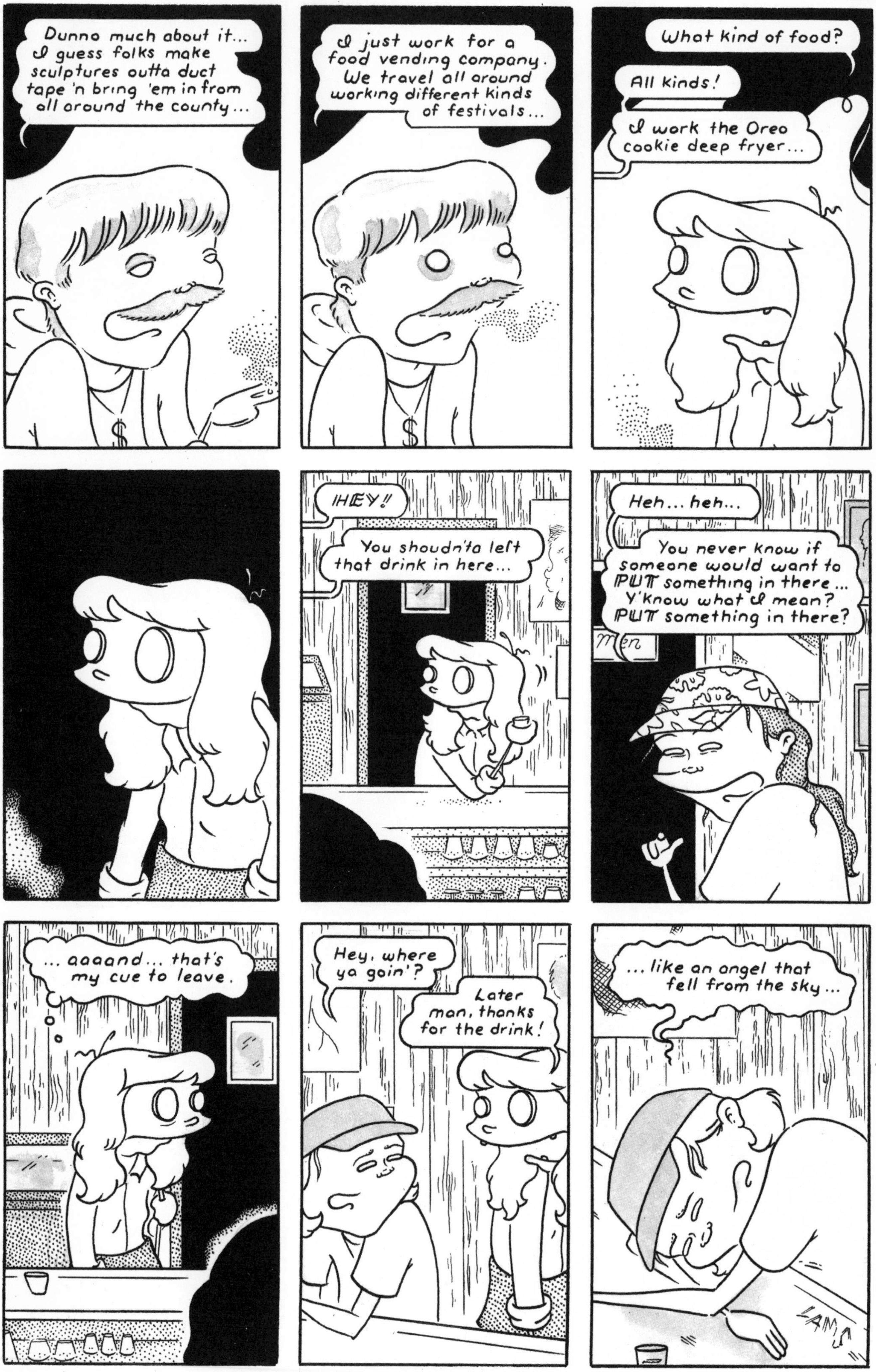

Dunno much about it... I guess folks make sculptures outta duct tape 'n bring 'em in from all around the county...
I just work for a food vending company. We travel all around working different kinds of festivals...
What kind of food?
All kinds!
I work the Oreo cookie deep fryer...
HEY!!
You shoudn'ta left that drink in here...
Heh... heh...
You never know if someone would want to PUT something in there... Y'know what I mean? PUT something in there?
Men
... aaaand... that's my cue to leave.
Hey, where ya goin'?
Later man, thanks for the drink!
... like an angel that fell from the sky...

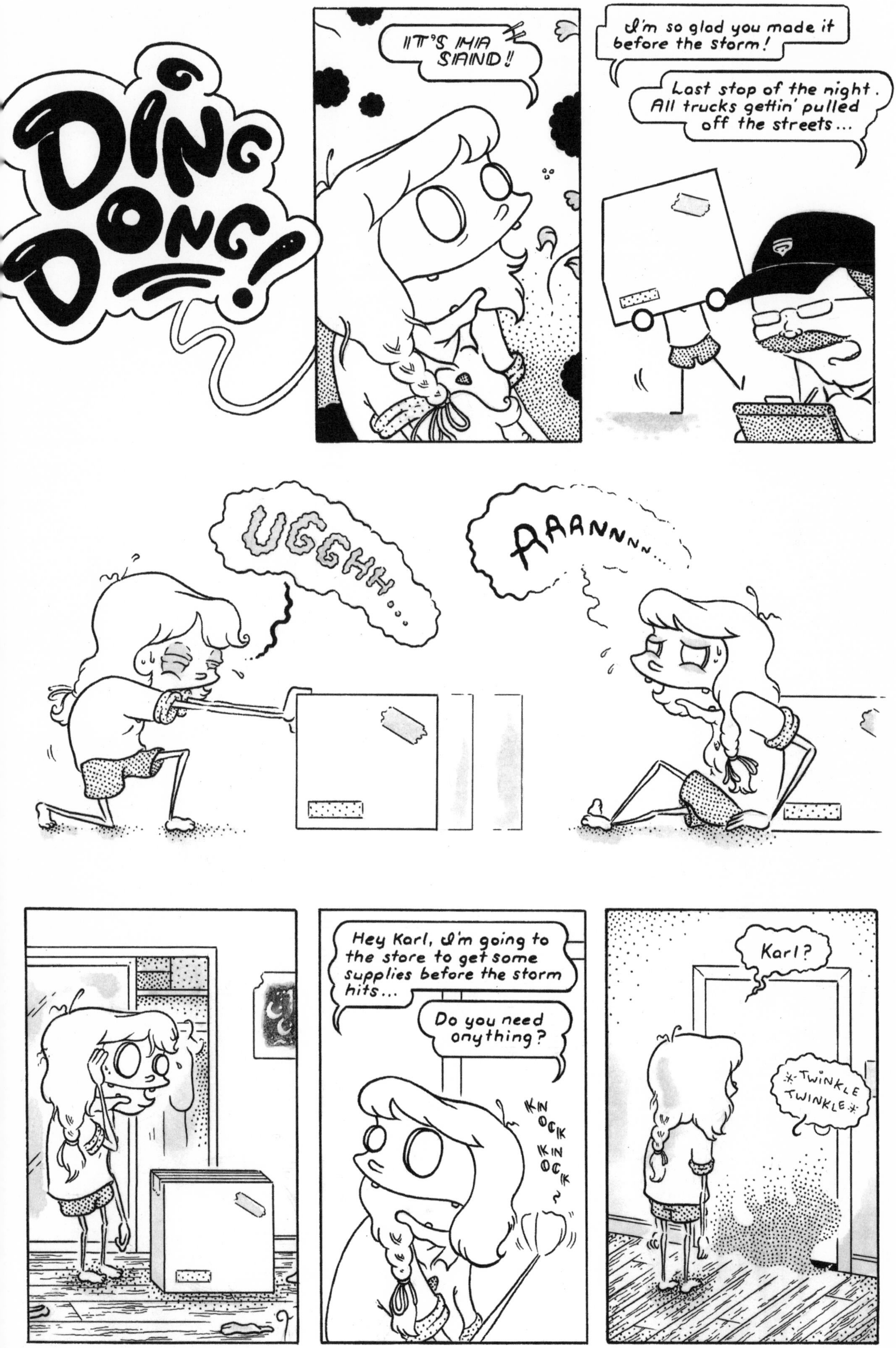
DING DONG!
IT'S IMA SIAND!!
I'm so glad you made it before the storm!
Last stop of the night. All trucks gettin' pulled off the streets...
UGGHH...
AAANNNN...
Hey Karl, I'm going to the store to get some supplies before the storm hits...
Do you need anything?
KNOCK KNOCK
Karl?
TWINKLE TWINKLE

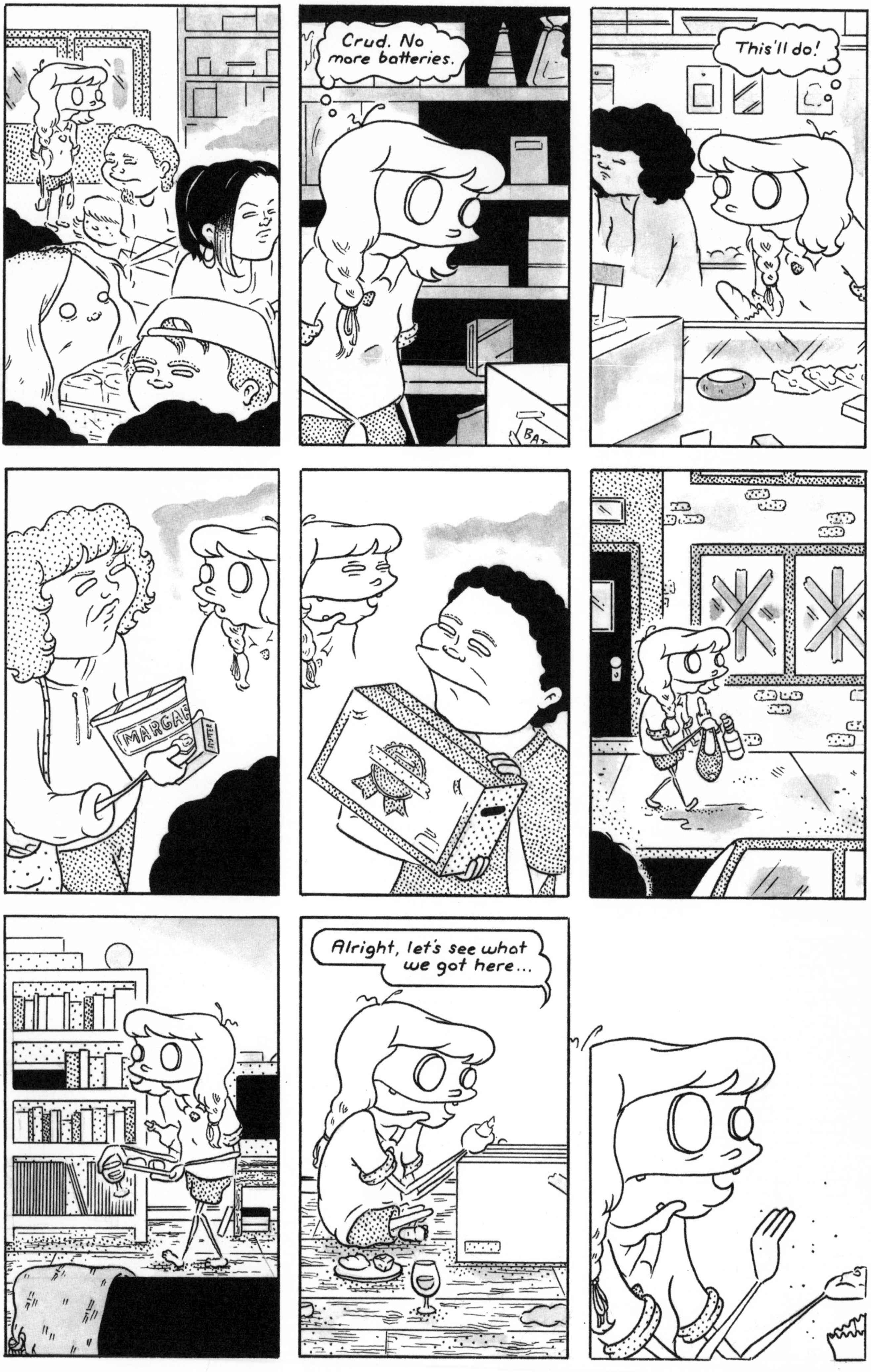

Crud. No more batteries.
This'll do!
Alright, let's see what we got here...

What IS that? GLASS?! A piece of GUM?!
Ugh!
It's all unusable!
I can't eat.
eep eep epp
Ring Ring...
BBRIIIING! BBRIIIING!
You've reached Larrybear, I'm not in... please leave a message...

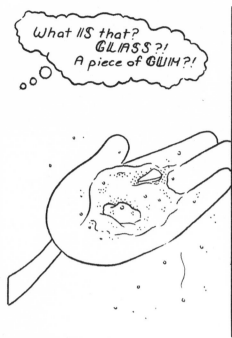

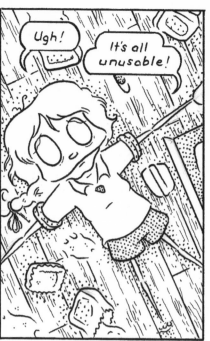

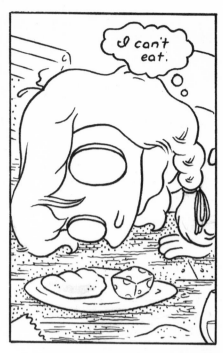

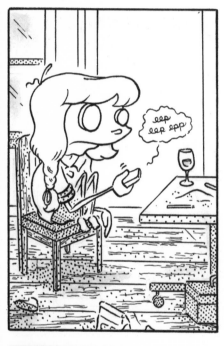

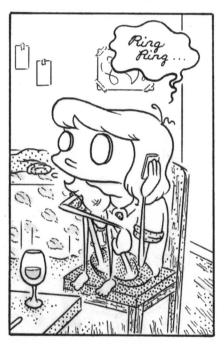

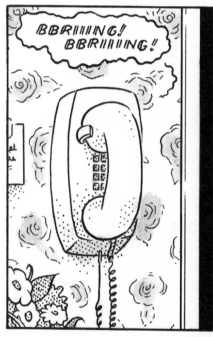

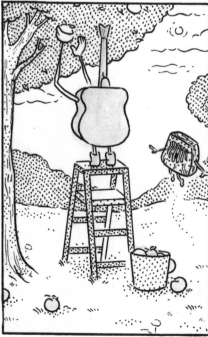

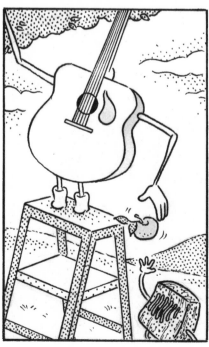

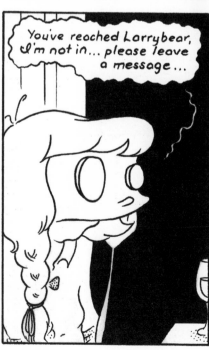

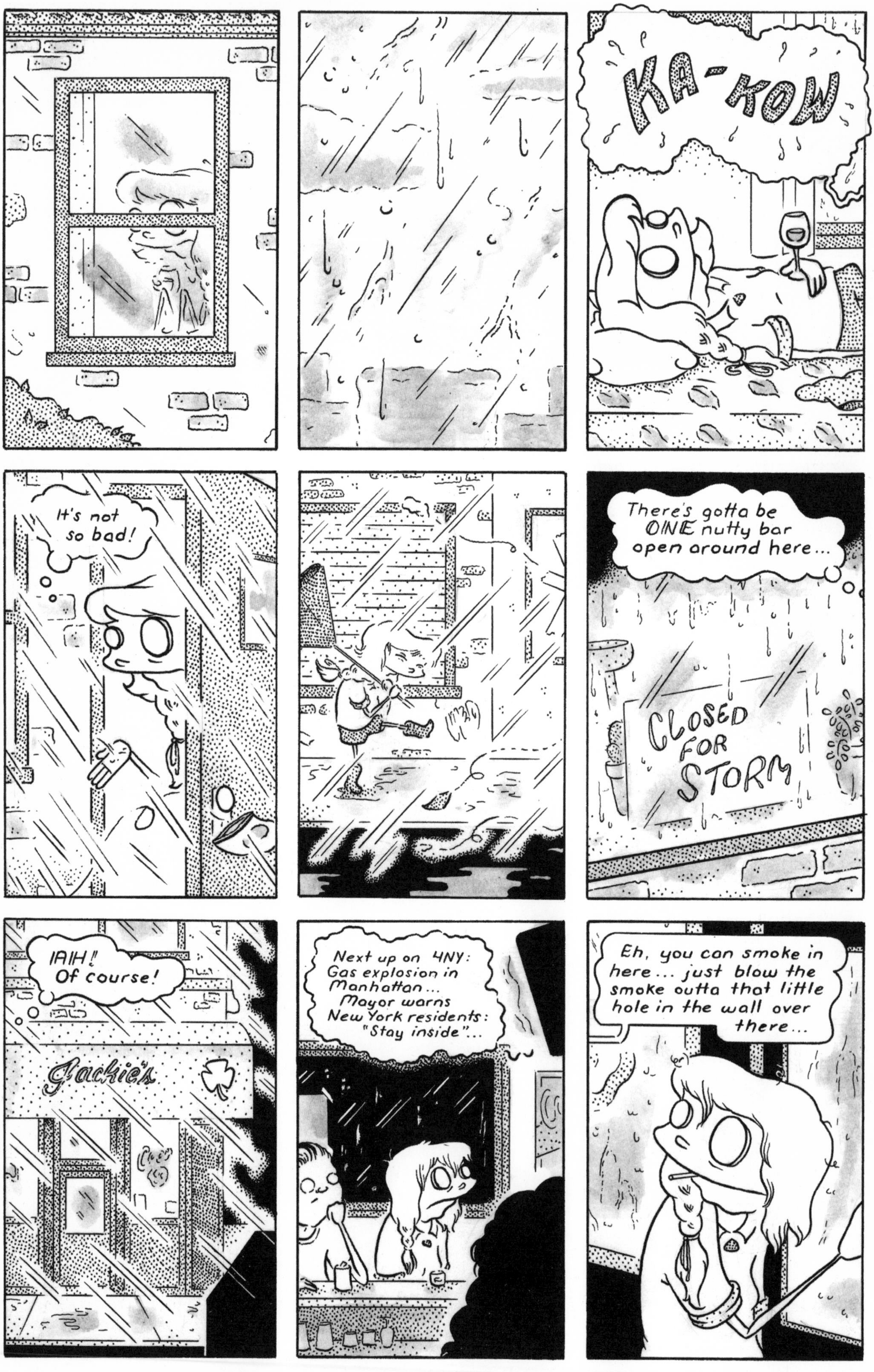
KA-KOW
It's not so bad!
There's gotta be ONE nutty bar open around here...
CLOSED FOR STORM
AH!! Of course!
Jackie's
Next up on 4NY: Gas explosion in Manhattan... Mayor warns New York residents: "Stay inside"...
Eh, you can smoke in here... just blow the smoke outta that little hole in the wall over there...

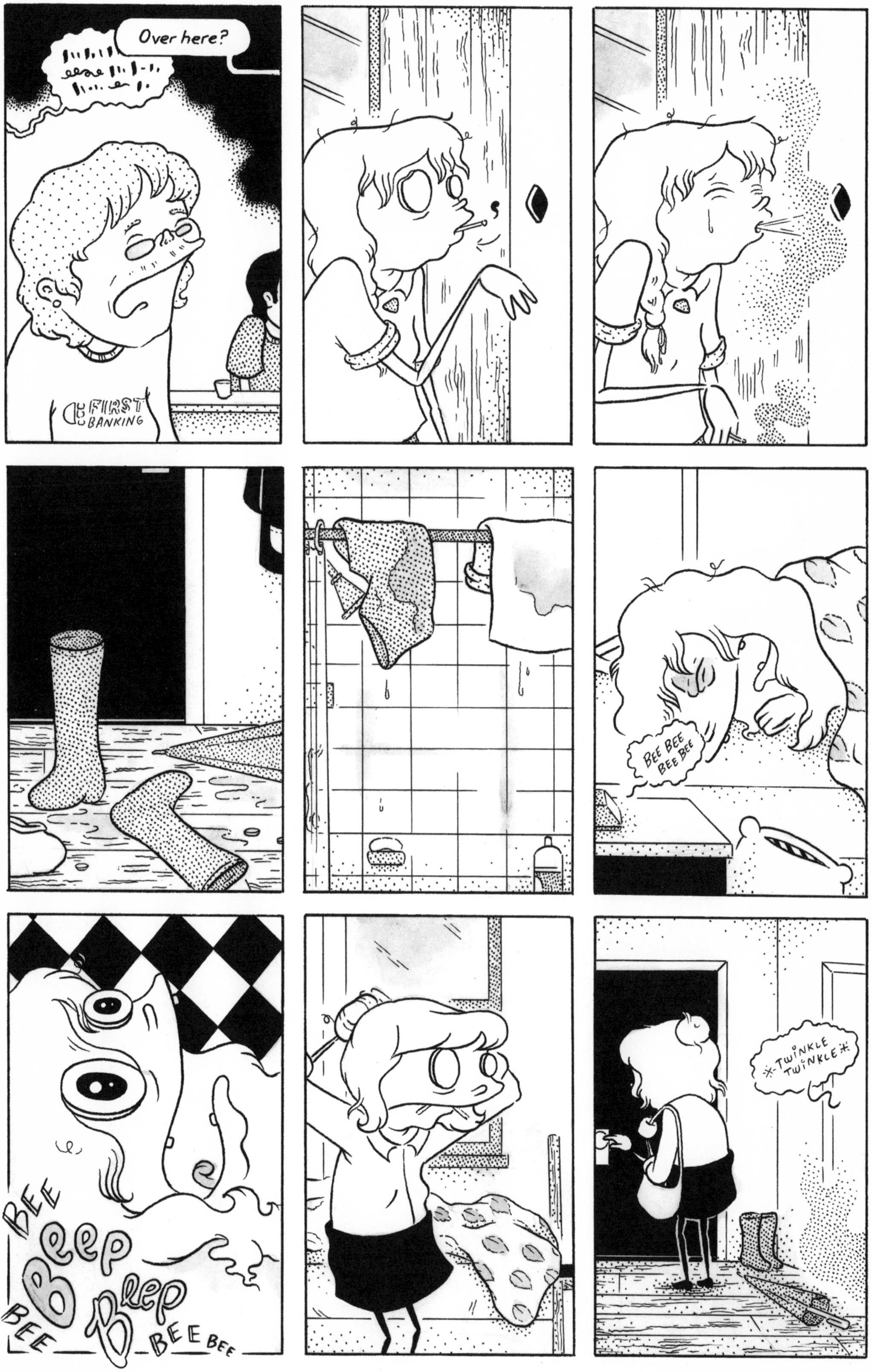
Over here?
FIRST BANKING
BEE BEE BEE BEE
BEE Beep BEE Bleep BEE BEE BEE
TWINKLE TWINKLE

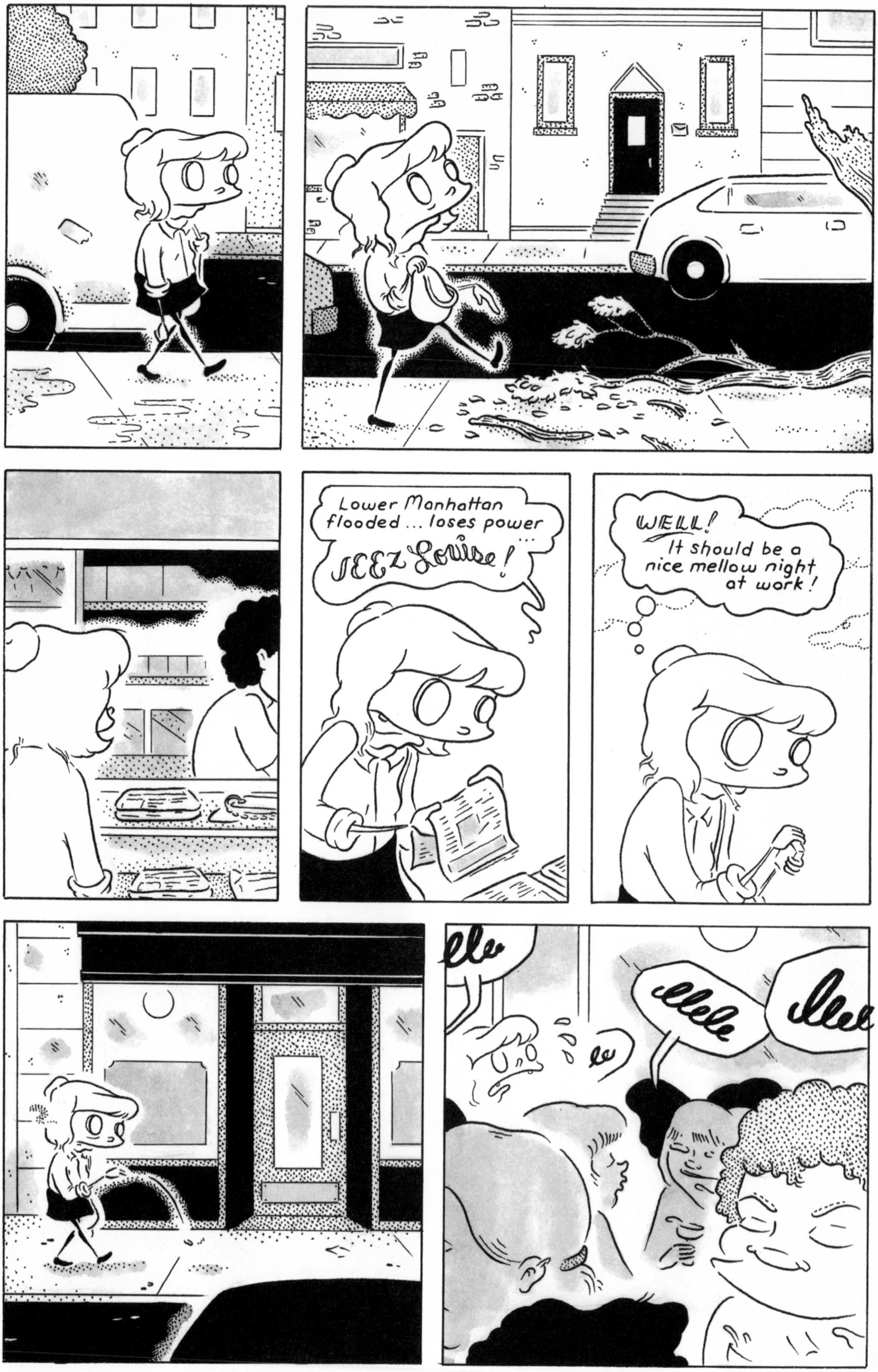
Lower Manhattan flooded ... loses power ...
JEEZ Louise!
WELL! It should be a nice mellow night at work!

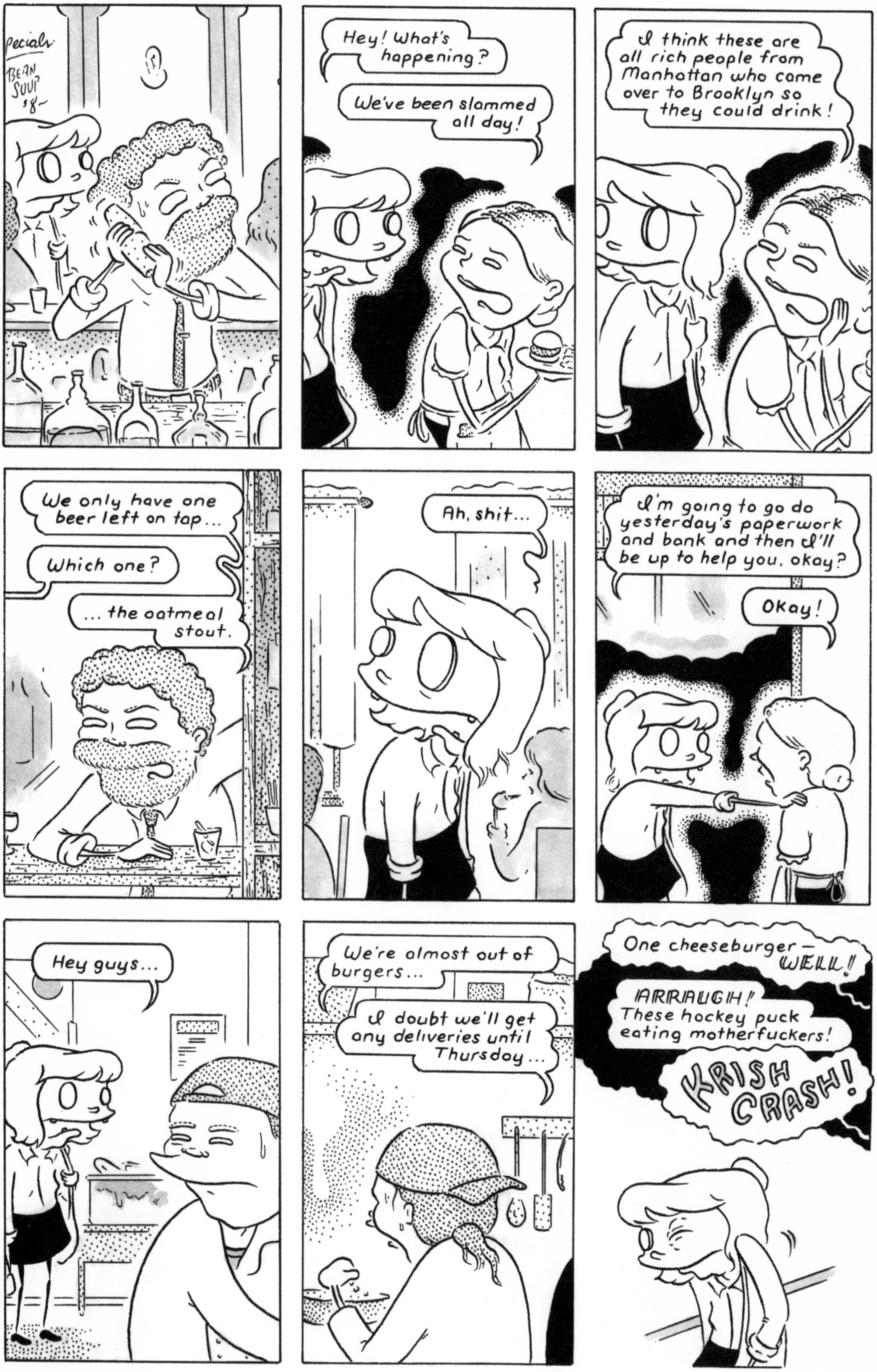
Specials
BEAN SOUP $8–
Hey! What's happening?
We've been slammed all day!
I think these are all rich people from Manhattan who came over to Brooklyn so they could drink!
We only have one beer left on tap...
Which one?
... the oatmeal stout.
Ah, shit...
I'm going to go do yesterday's paperwork and bank and then I'll be up to help you, okay?
Okay!
Hey guys...
We're almost out of burgers...
I doubt we'll get any deliveries until Thursday...
One cheeseburger— WELL!
ARRAUGH! These hockey puck eating motherfuckers!
KRISH CRASH!

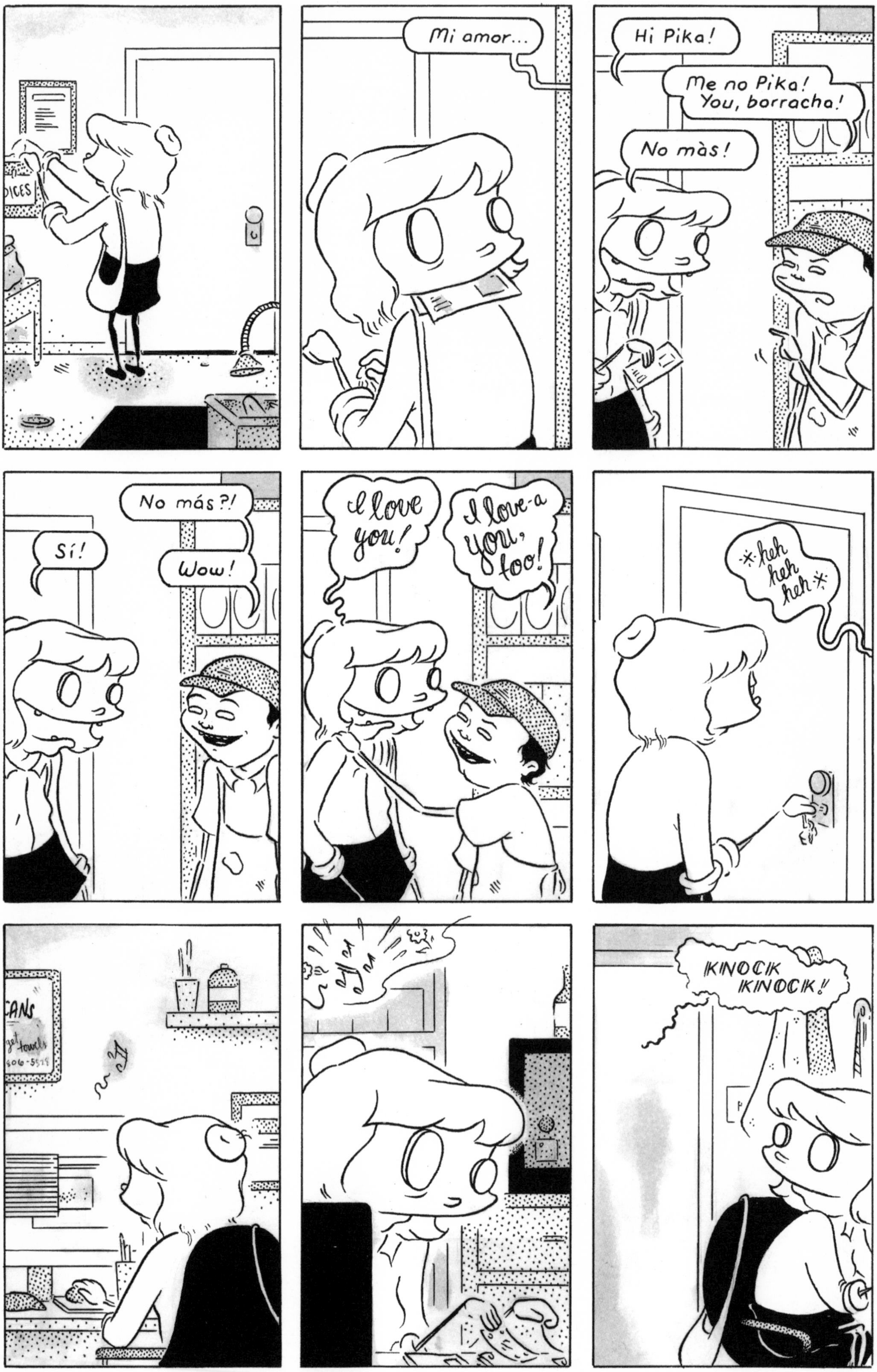
Mi amor...
Hi Pika!
Me no Pika! You, borracha!
No màs!
Sí!
No más?!
Wow!
I love you!
I love-a you, too!
heh heh heh
KNOCK KNOCK!

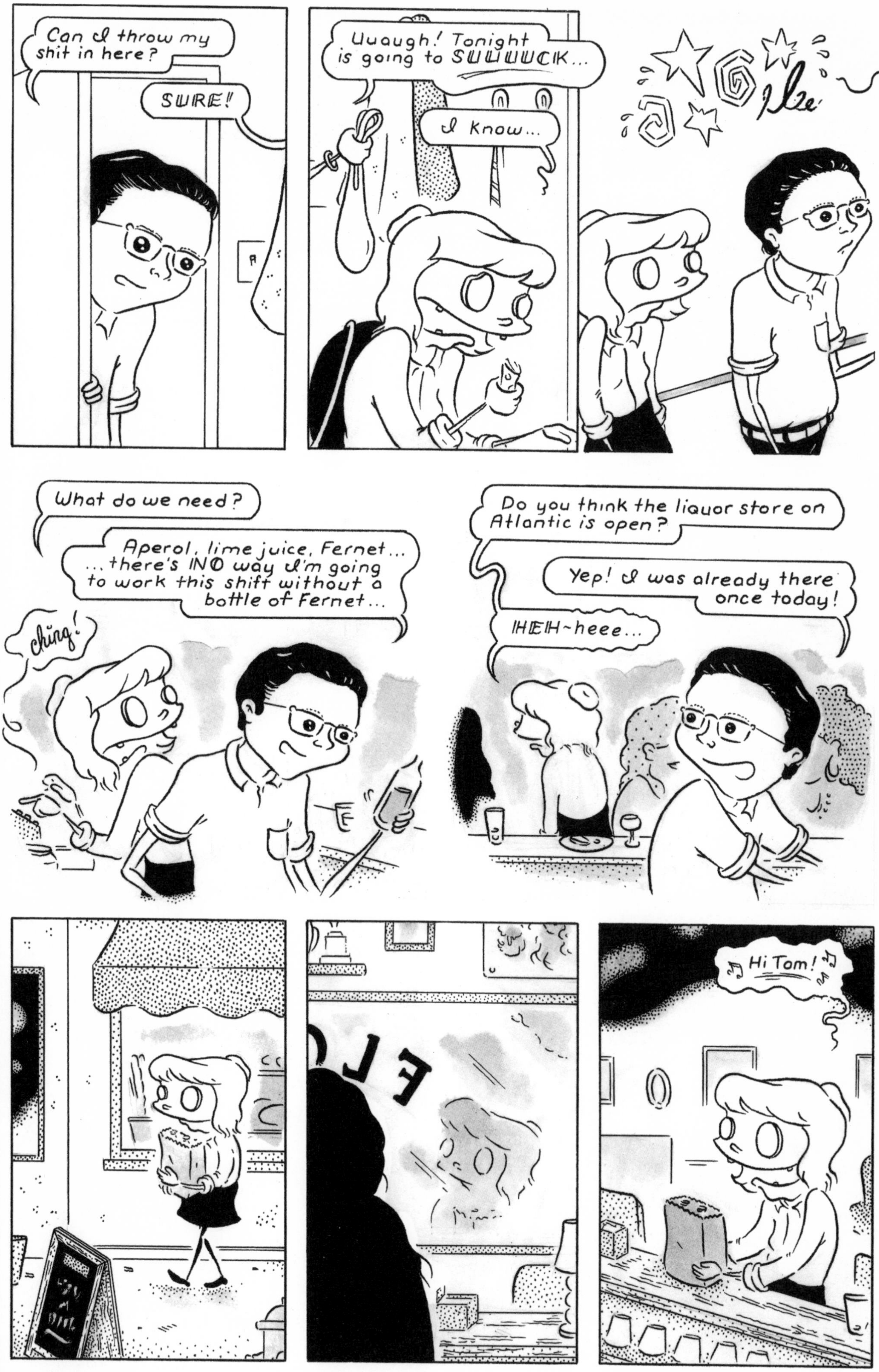
Can I throw my shit in here?
SURE!
Uuaugh! Tonight is going to SUUUUCK...
I know...
What do we need?
Aperol, lime juice, Fernet... ...there's NO way I'm going to work this shift without a bottle of Fernet...
ching!
Do you think the liquor store on Atlantic is open?
Yep! I was already there once today!
HEH~heee...
Hi Tom!

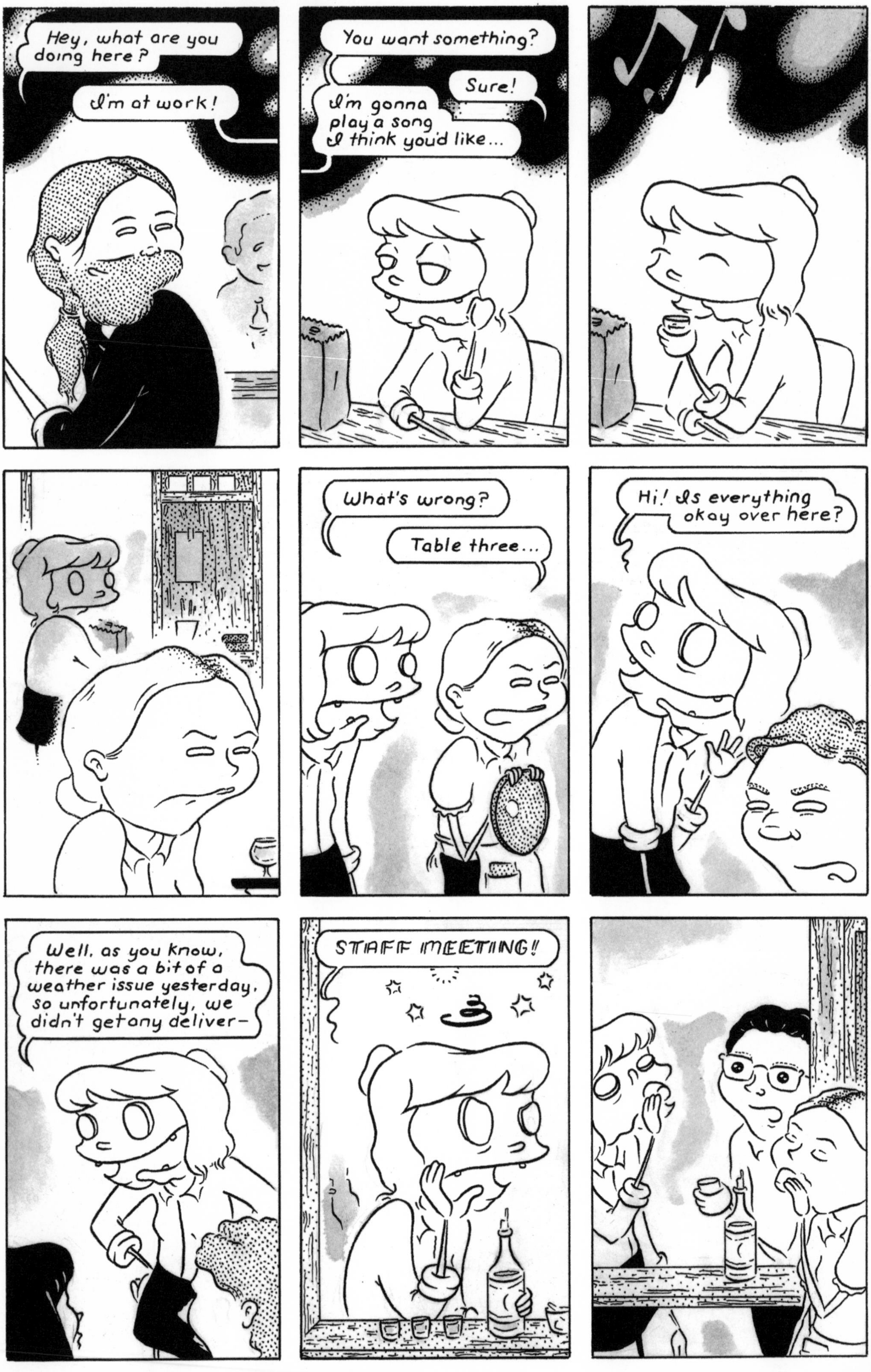
Hey, what are you doing here?
I'm at work!
You want something?
Sure!
I'm gonna play a song I think you'd like...
What's wrong?
Table three...
Hi! Is everything okay over here?
Well, as you know, there was a bit of a weather issue yesterday, so unfortunately, we didn't get any deliver-
STAFF MEETING!

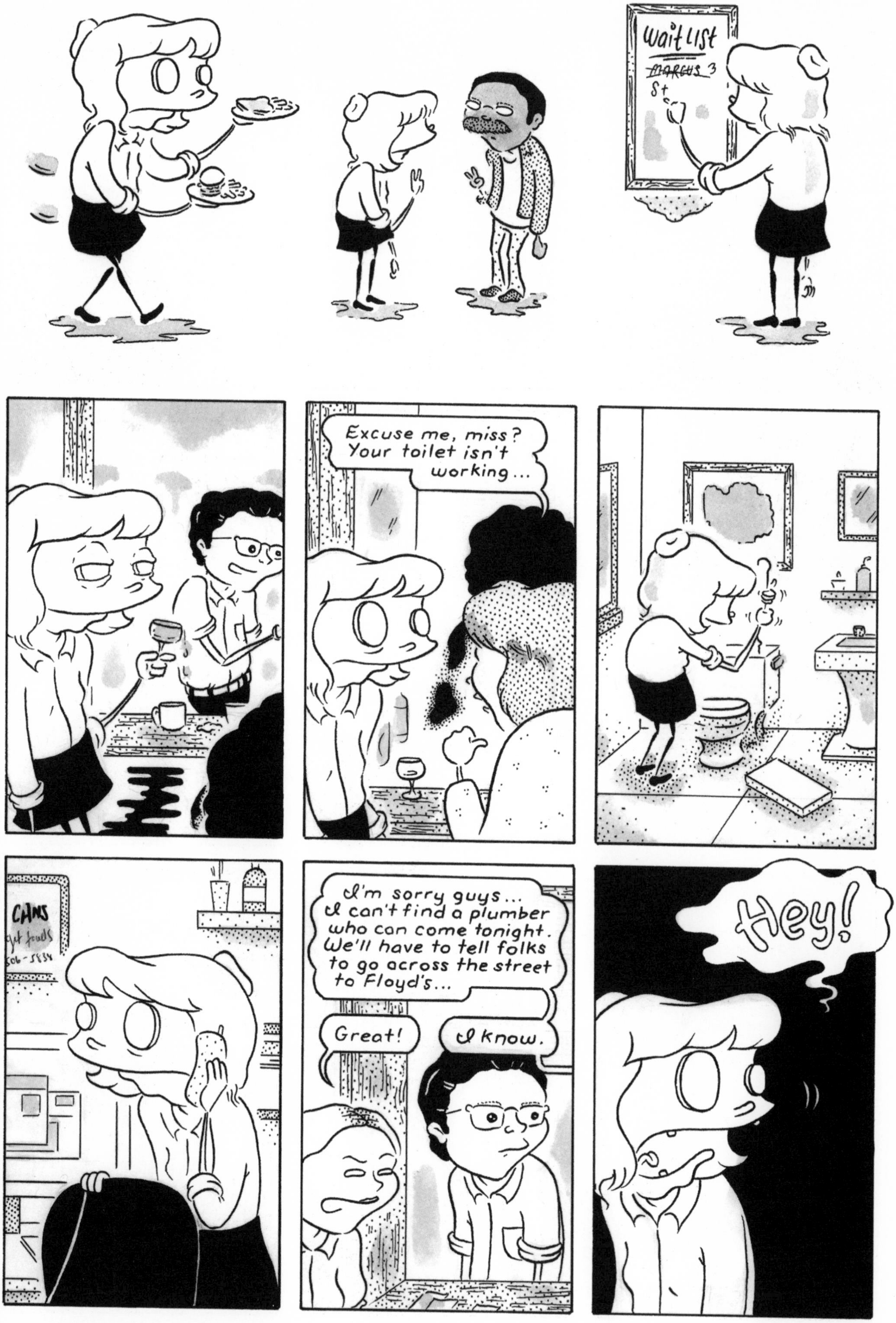
wait LIST
Excuse me, miss? Your toilet isn't working...
I'm sorry guys... I can't find a plumber who can come tonight. We'll have to tell folks to go across the street to Floyd's...
Great!
I know.
Hey!

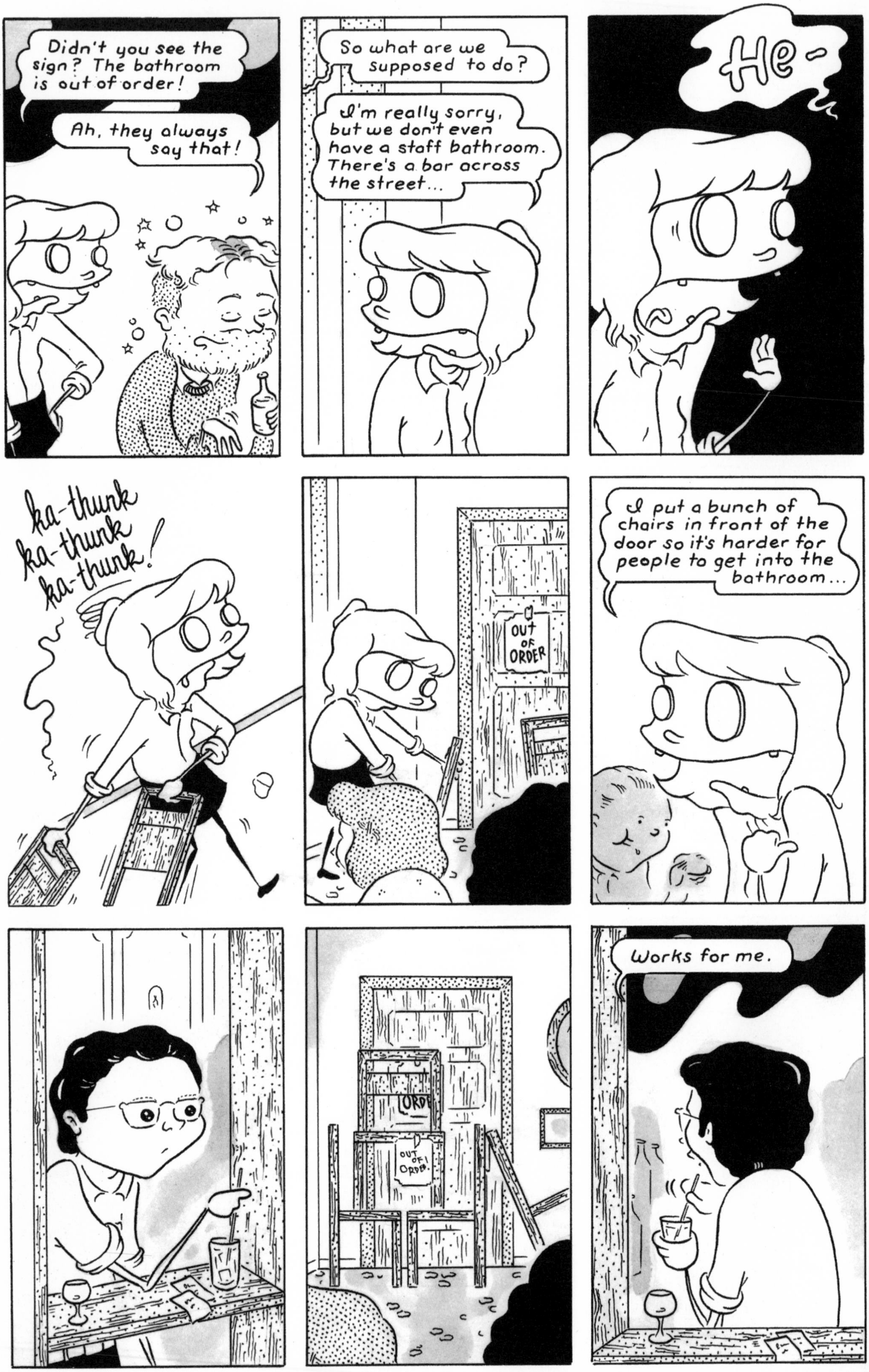
Didn't you see the sign? The bathroom is out of order!
Ah, they always say that!
So what are we supposed to do?
I'm really sorry, but we don't even have a staff bathroom. There's a bar across the street...
He-
ka-thunk ka-thunk ka-thunk!
OUT OF ORDER
I put a bunch of chairs in front of the door so it's harder for people to get into the bathroom...
OUT OF ORDER!
Works for me.

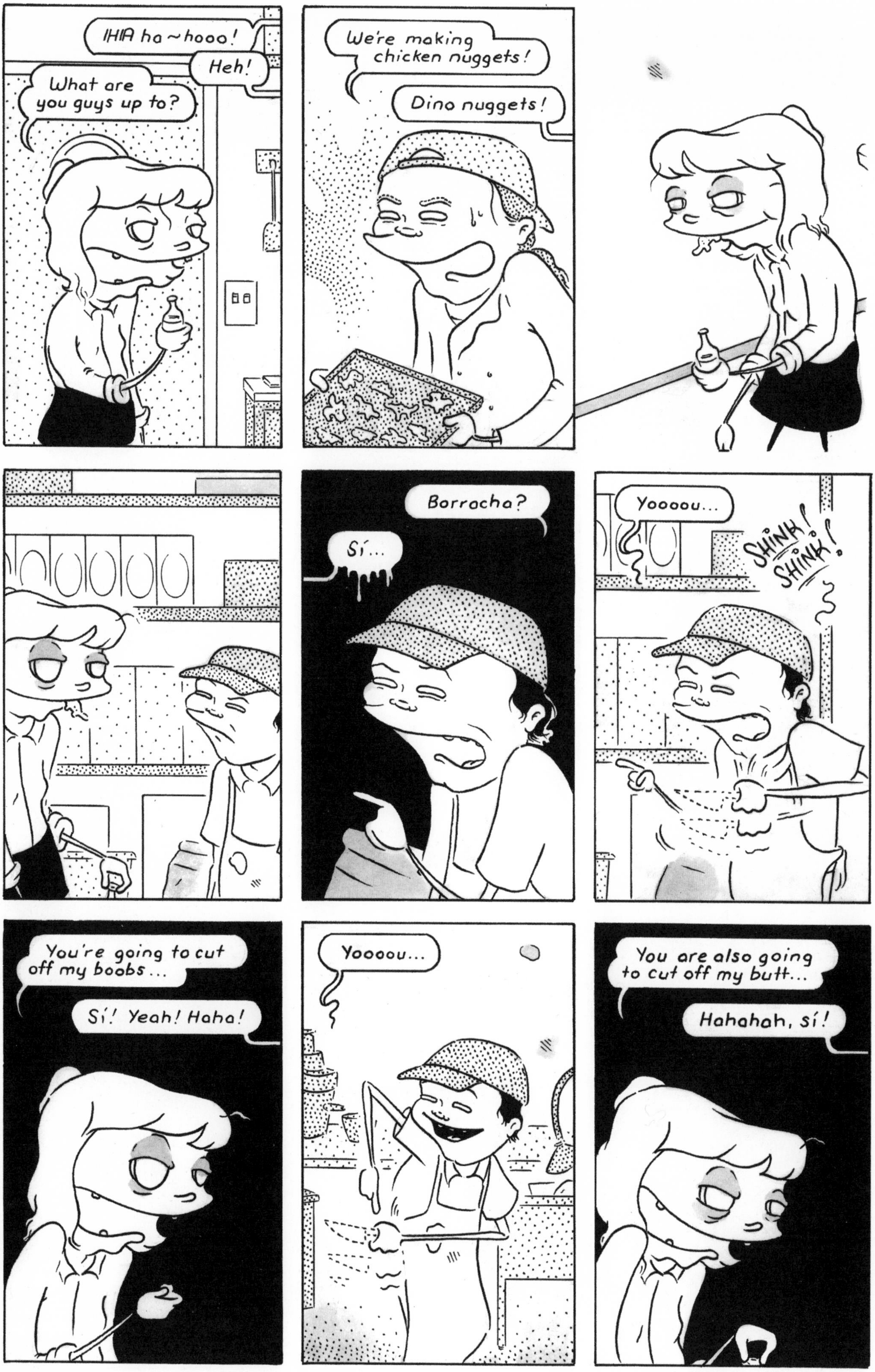
IHIA ha~hooo!
Heh!
What are you guys up to?
We're making chicken nuggets!
Dino nuggets!
Borracha?
Sí...
Yooou...
SHINK! SHINK!
You're going to cut off my boobs...
Sí! Yeah! Haha!
Yooou...
You are also going to cut off my butt...
Hahahah, sí!

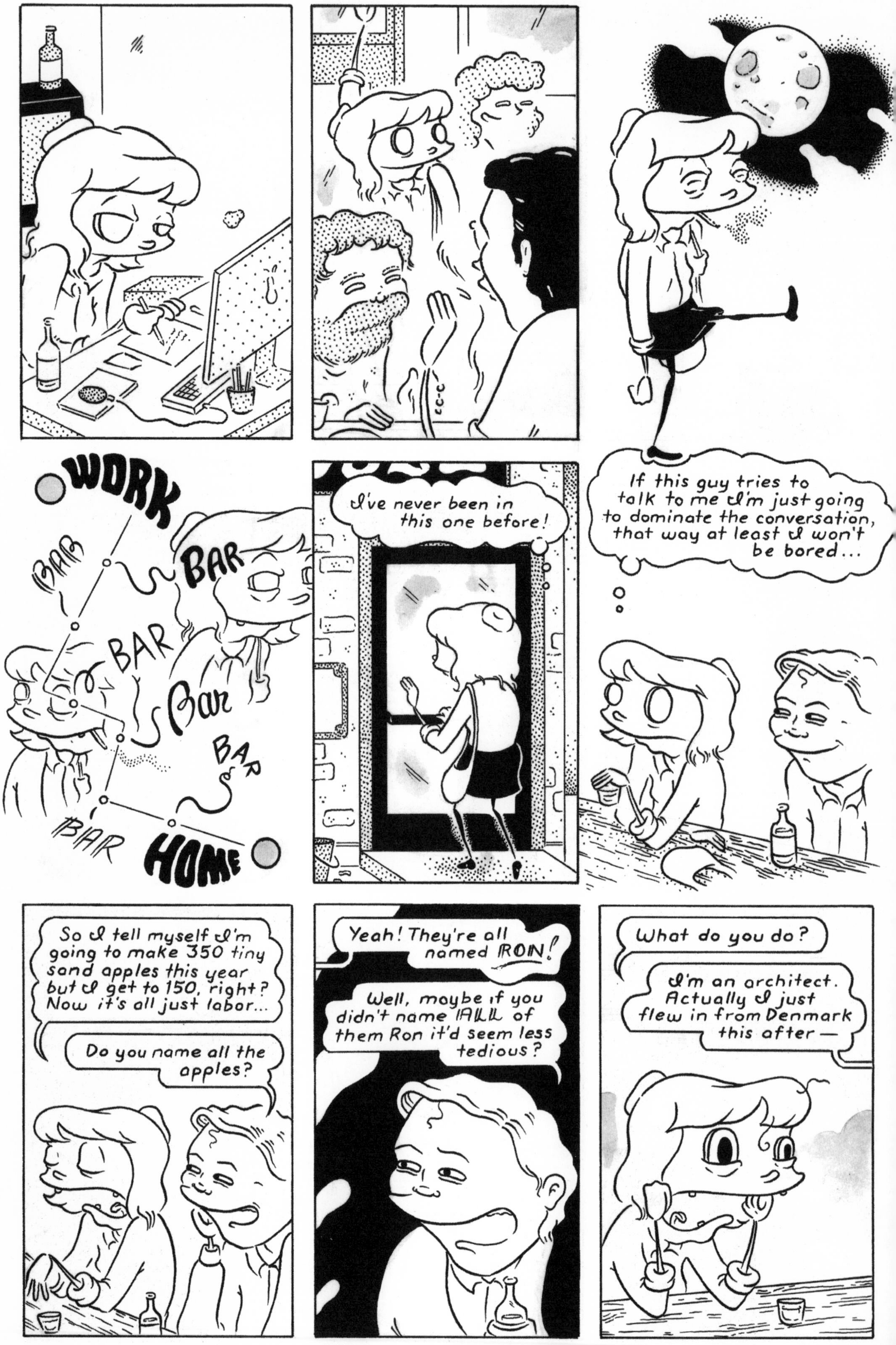
WORK
BAR
BAR
BAR
Bar
BAR
BAR
HOME
I've never been in this one before!
If this guy tries to talk to me I'm just going to dominate the conversation, that way at least I won't be bored...
So I tell myself I'm going to make 350 tiny sand apples this year but I get to 150, right? Now it's all just labor...
Do you name all the apples?
Yeah! They're all named RON!
Well, maybe if you didn't name ALL of them Ron it'd seem less tedious?
What do you do?
I'm an architect. Actually I just flew in from Denmark this after—

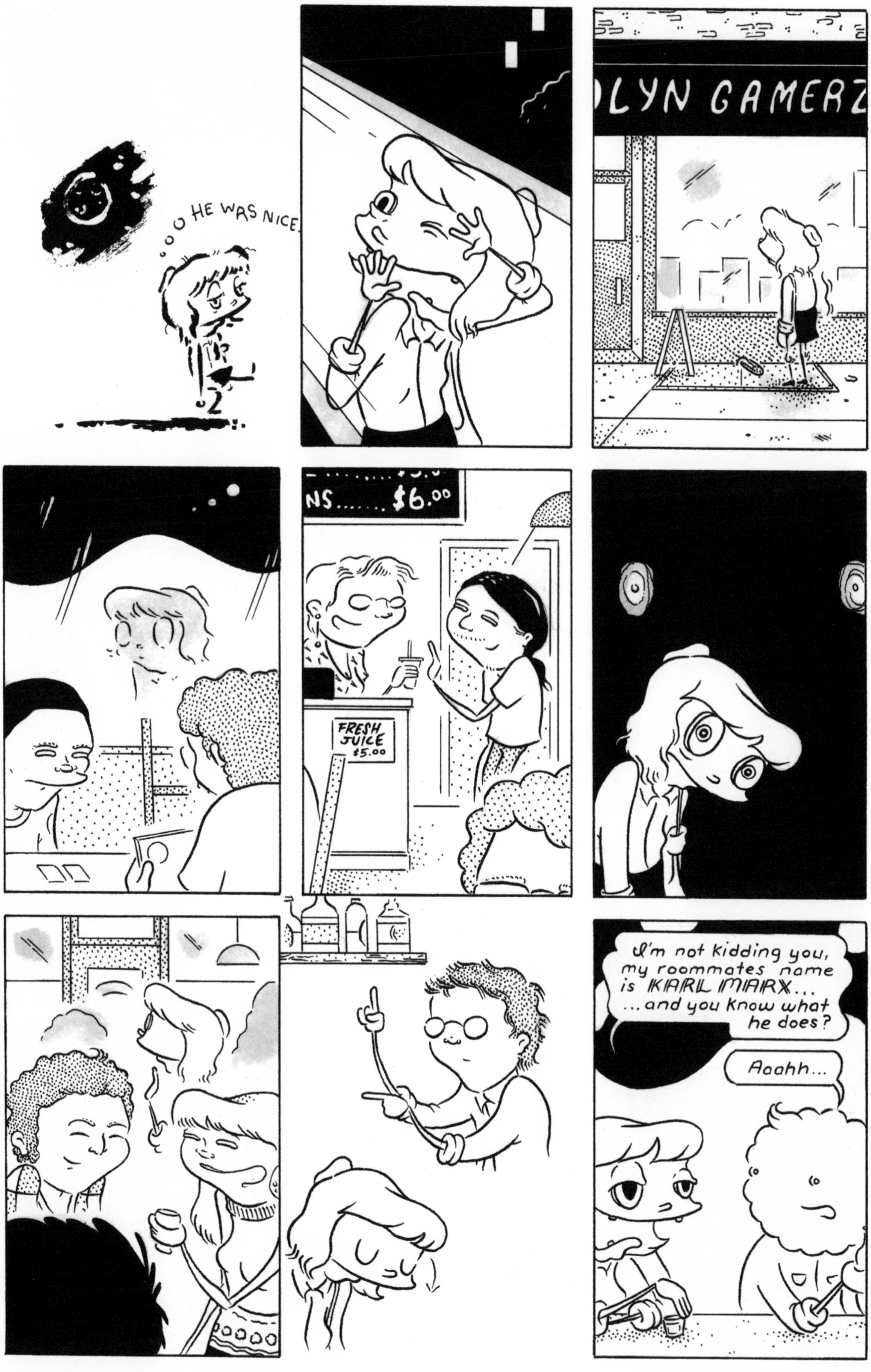

HE WAS NICE.
OLYN GAMERZ
NS....... $6.00
FRESH JUICE $5.00
I'm not kidding you, my roommates name is KARL MARX... ...and you know what he does?
Aaahh...

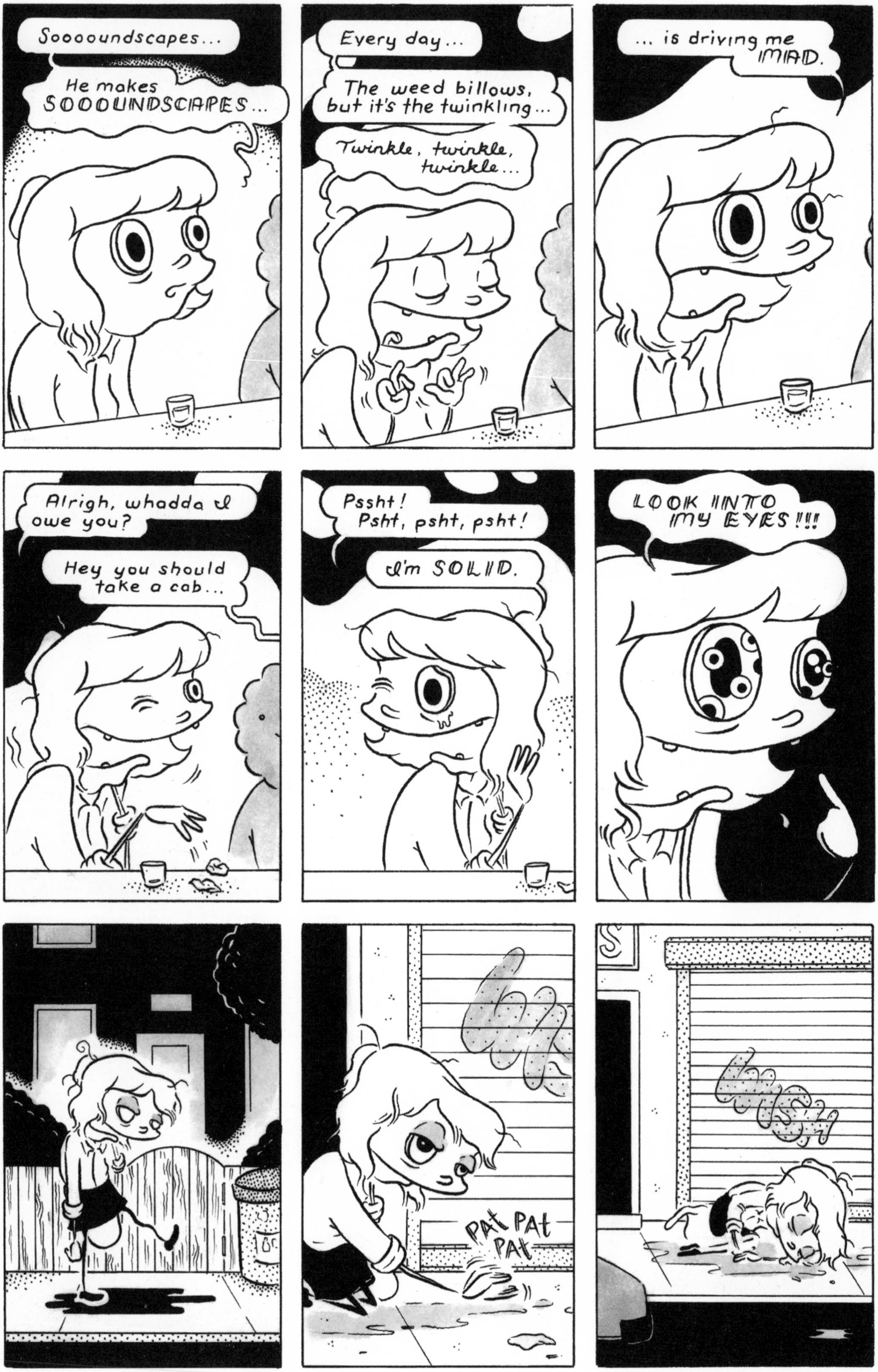

Soooooundscapes...
He makes SOOOUNDSCAPES...
Every day...
The weed billows, but it's the twinkling...
Twinkle, twinkle, twinkle...
... is driving me MAD.
Alrigh, whadda I owe you?
Hey you should take a cab...
Pssht! Psht, psht, psht!
I'm SOLID.
LOOK INTO MY EYES!!!
PAT PAT PAT

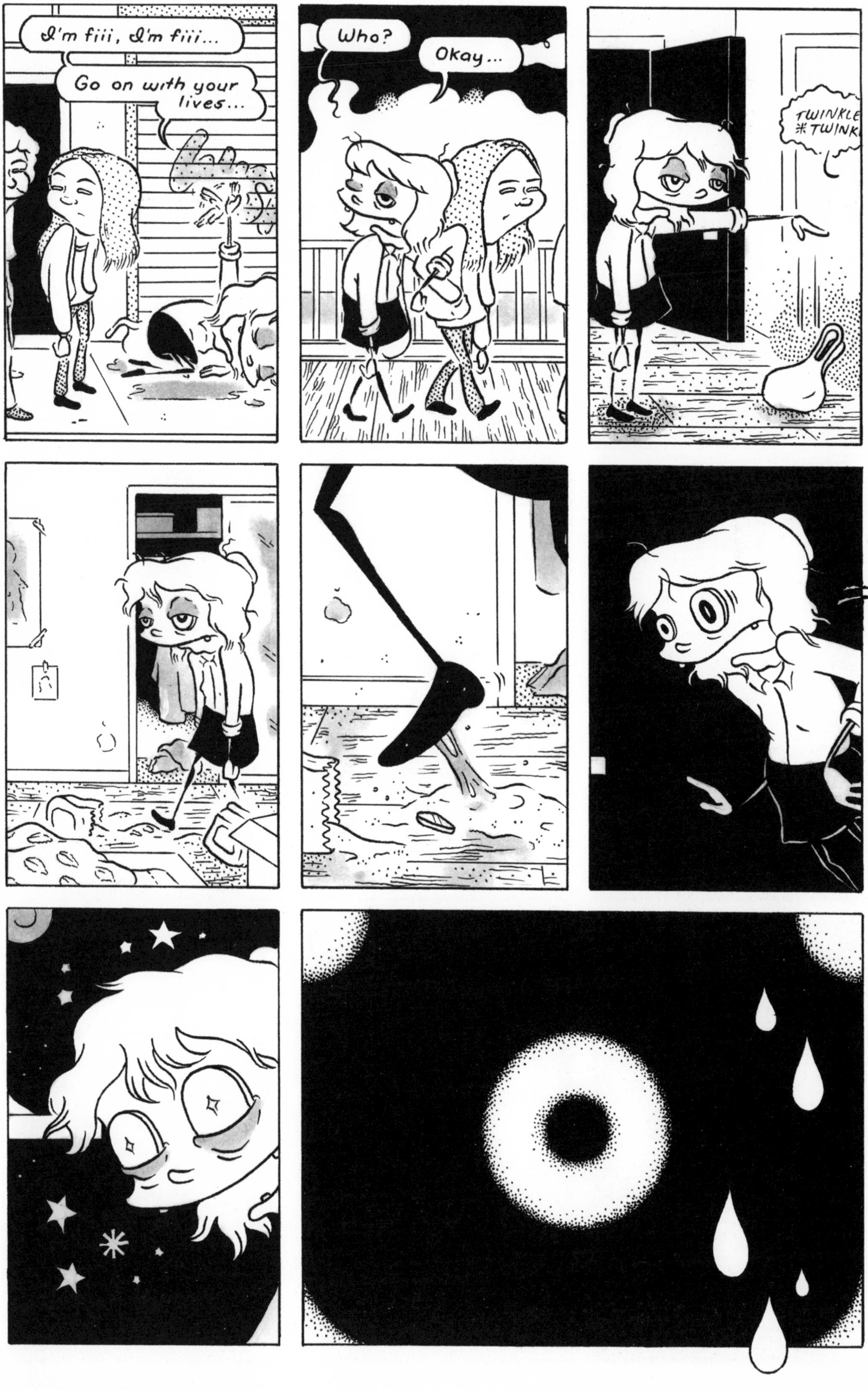
I'm fiii, I'm fiii...
Go on with your lives...
Who?
Okay...
TWINKLE
* TWINKL

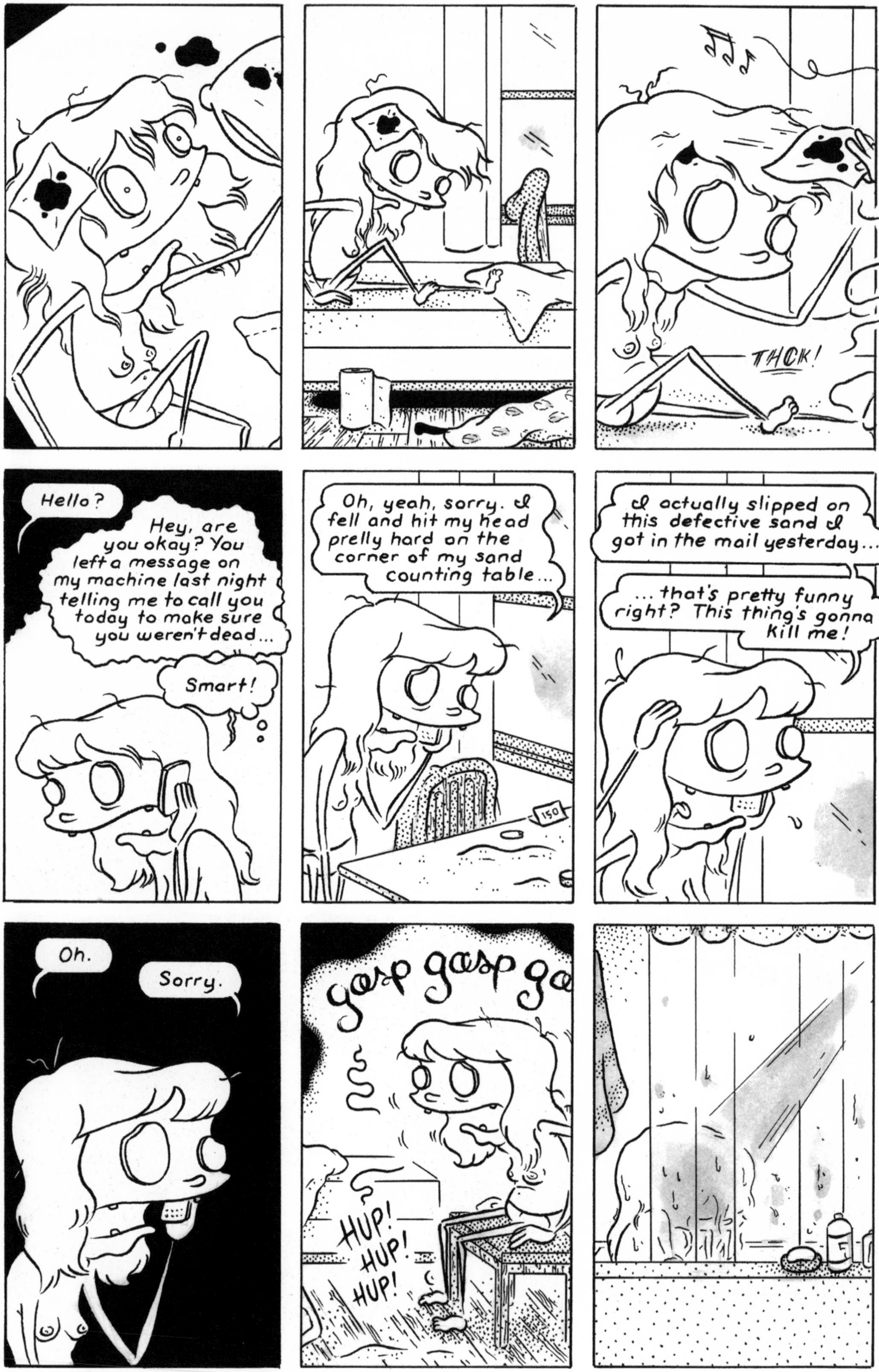

THCK!
Hello?
Hey, are you okay? You left a message on my machine last night telling me to call you today to make sure you weren't dead...
Smart!
Oh, yeah, sorry. I fell and hit my head pretty hard on the corner of my sand counting table...
150
I actually slipped on this defective sand I got in the mail yesterday...
... that's pretty funny right? This thing's gonna kill me!
Oh.
Sorry.
gasp gasp ga
HUP!
HUP!
HUP!

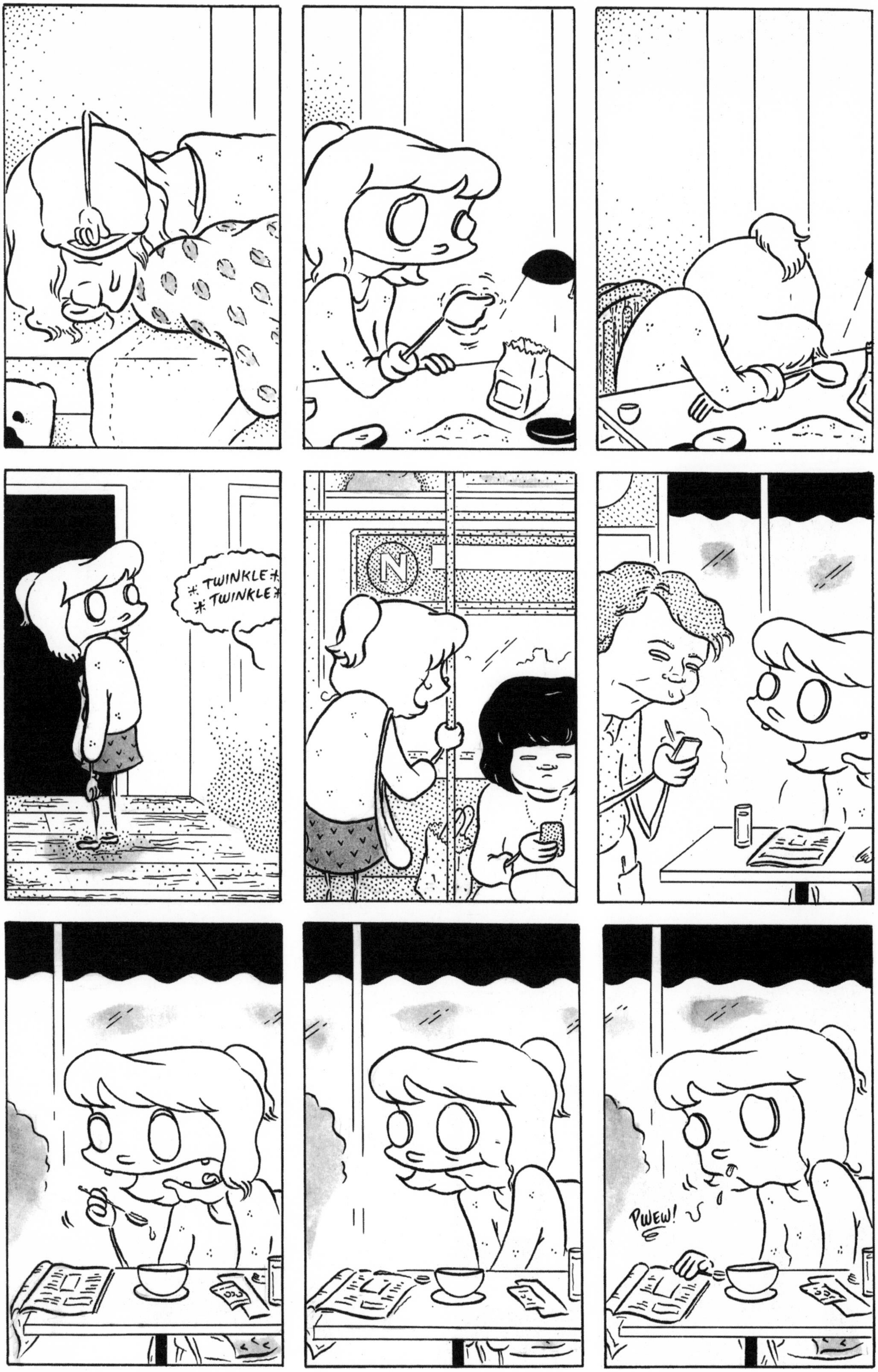
* TWINKLE * * TWINKLE *
PWEW!

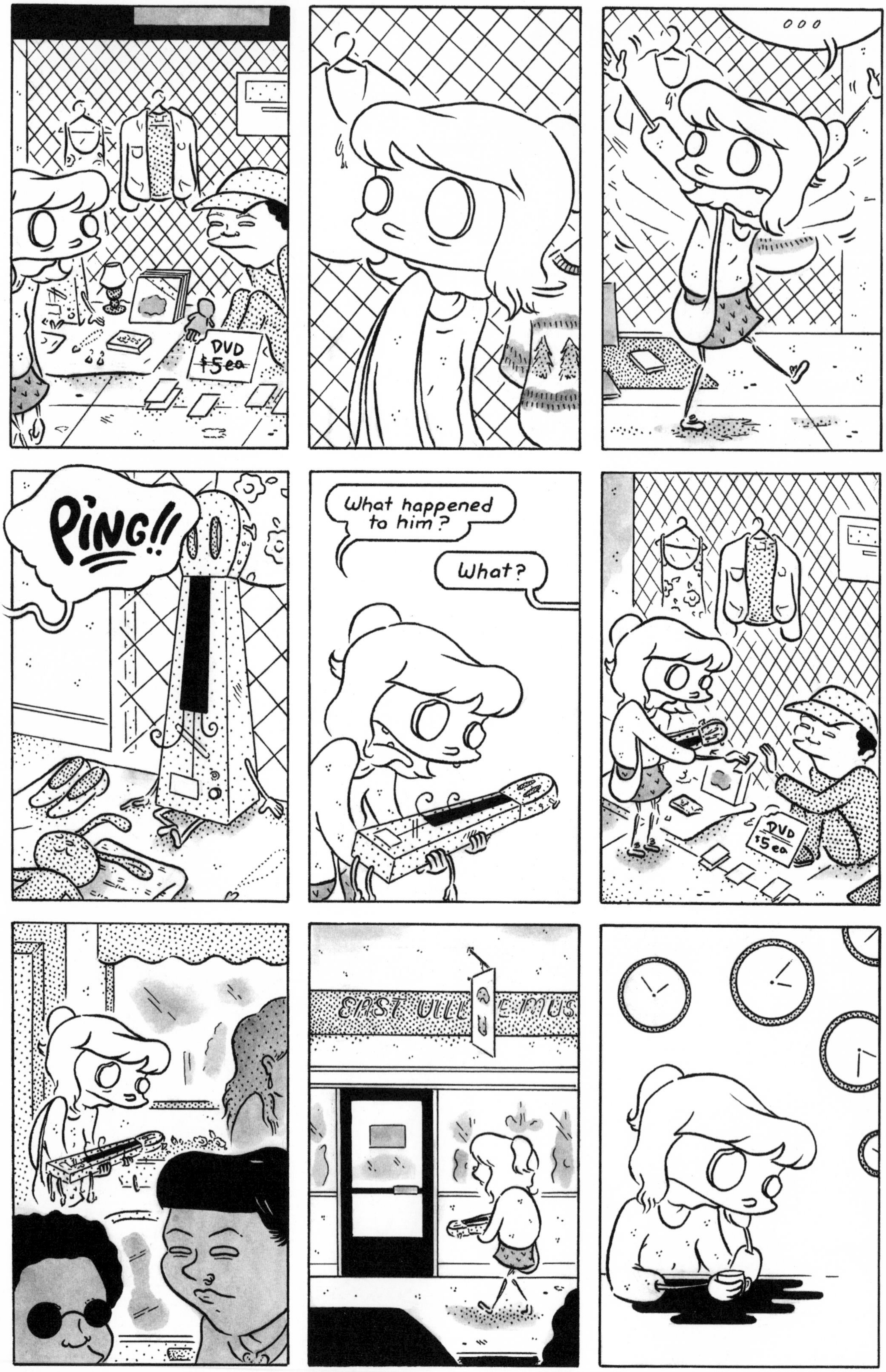

DVD
$5ea
ooo
PING!!
What happened to him?
What?
DVD
$5ea
EAST VILL E MUS

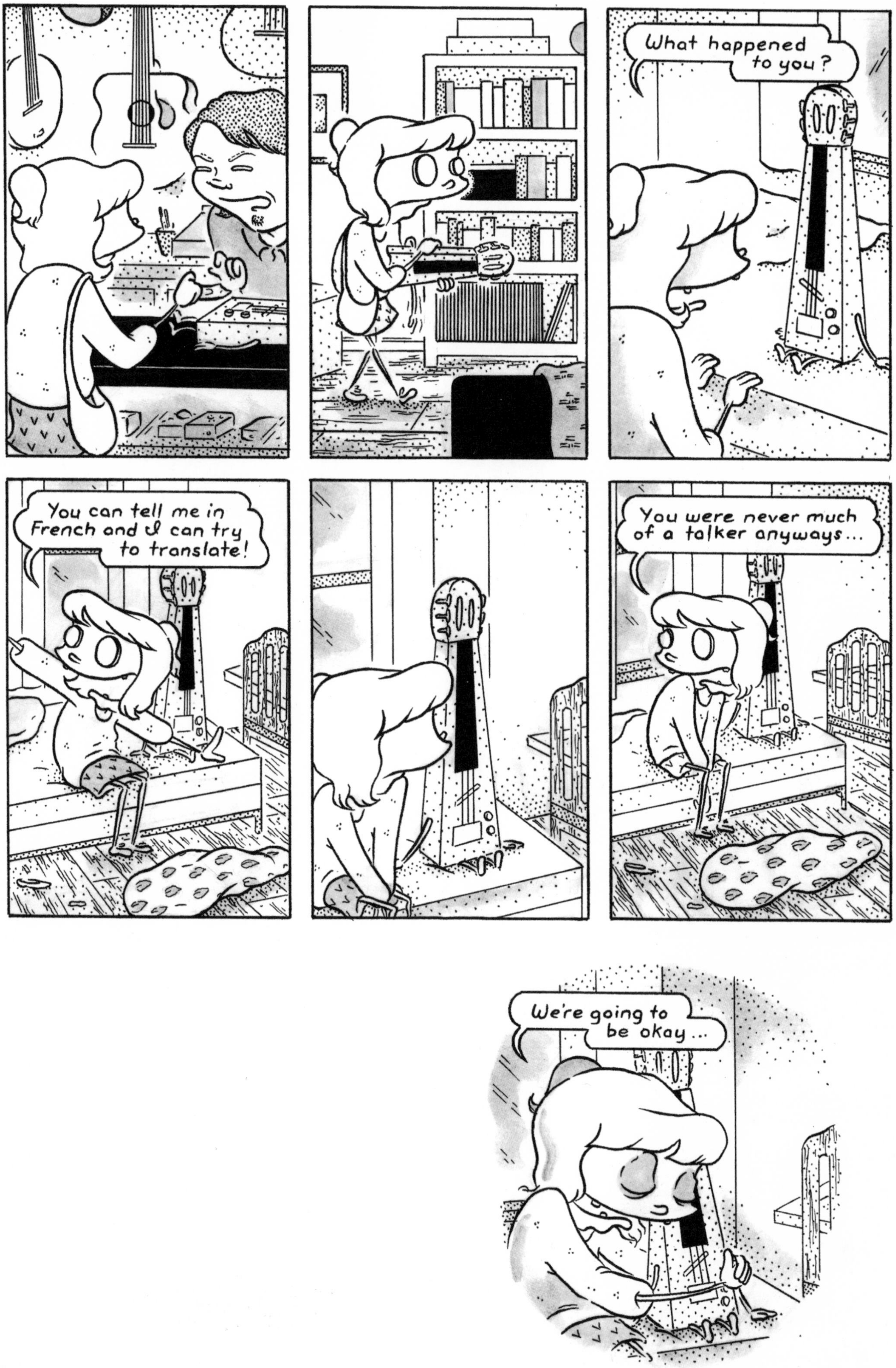
What happened to you?
You can tell me in French and I can try to translate!
You were never much of a talker anyways...
We're going to be okay...

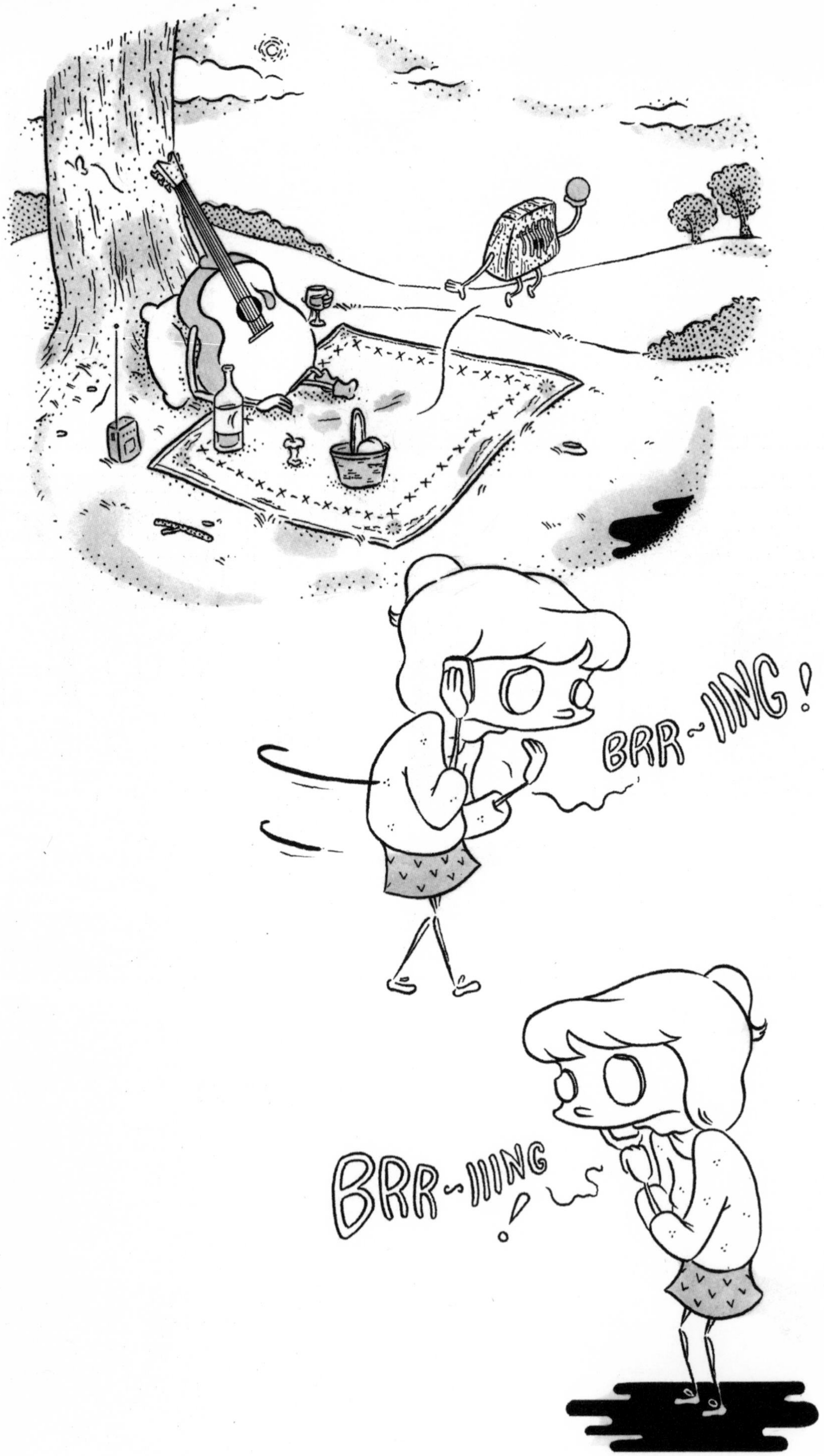
BRR~IING!
BRR~IIING!

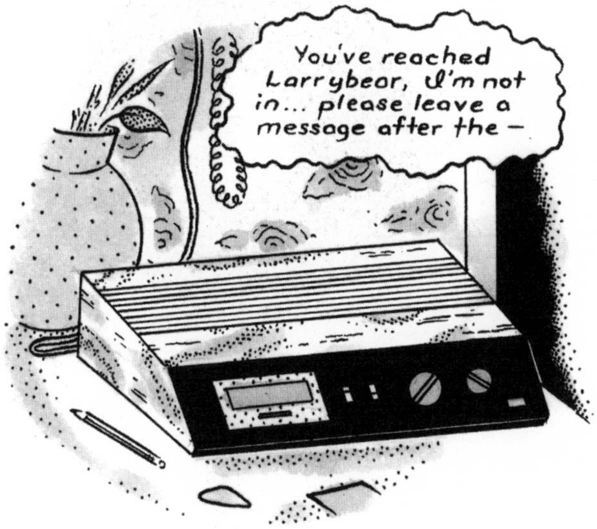
You've reached Larrybear, I'm not in... please leave a message after the–

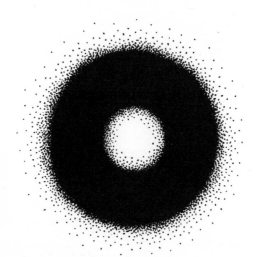